LESSONS OF EXPERIENCE OF A GE CFO

Jay Braukman

Copyright © 2018 Jay Braukman
All rights reserved
First Edition

NEWMAN SPRINGS PUBLISHING
320 Broad Street
Red Bank, NJ 07701

First originally published by Newman Springs Publishing 2018

ISBN 978-1-64096-355-9 (Paperback)
ISBN 978-1-64096-356-6 (Hardcover)
ISBN 978-1-64096-357-3 (Digital)

Printed in the United States of America

CONTENTS

Acknowledgments 5
Introduction 7
Chapter 1: Growing Up 9
Chapter 2: The College Years 28
Chapter 3: Joining GE 40
Chapter 4: Computerized Tomography 45
Chapter 5: The Audit Staff 50
Chapter 6: Video Products 83
Chapter 7: Coshocton, Ohio 87
Chapter 8: Diamonds 93
Chapter 9: GE Programs Finance 103
Chapter 10: Aircraft Engines 109
Chapter 11: The Eddie Russell Affair 116
Chapter 12: Six Sigma 123
Chapter 13: From Planes to Trains 126
Chapter 14: Developing GE leaders 135
Chapter 15: Nuovo Pignone, Italy 141
Chapter 16: Divorce 157
Chapter 17: Officer Assessment Process 162
Chapter 18: "Motor's Plus" 164
Chapter 19: IT Solutions 168
Chapter 20: Concluding Thoughts 178

ACKNOWLEDGMENTS

I would like to thank Jack Welch, Dennis Dammerman, and Paolo Fresco for their guidance, leadership, and opportunities given to me during my twenty-three-year career in GE. Also, to all the presidents and executives of businesses or functions for their friendship, leadership, and mentoring. In addition, to all employees and peers for your commitment and coaching to make me a better leader. It was greatly appreciated, and I hope you learned a lot from our joint experiences. Last, to my wife, Nicky, and professors who encouraged me to write this book.

INTRODUCTION

As Stephen H. Baum writes in his book *What Made Jack Welch*, he states, "I began to see a pattern of life experiences that, remarkably, all had undergone. I came to see that it was an accumulation of all these experiences that had encouraged and made possible their extraordinary personal growth. In spite of differences in age, gender, location, education, and more, they all recollected critical moments in their lives that stimulated personal growth and sharpened their desires and their abilities—moments that helped shape them into leaders."

These are my experiences.

CHAPTER 1

Growing Up

Early in life, I attended Catholic schools in kindergarten and the first, second, third, and fourth grade. Having to learn from the nuns is a special opportunity. I didn't know of one that didn't have a ruler. They were incredibly strict, and if you weren't listening or, God forbid, dozing off or passing notes the punishment was always a smack across the hand with that ruler. In kindergarten, the nuns insisted that they call me John, which is my given name, but every one called me Jay because my grandfather was John and my dad was John Jr. It kept things from being confusing. Well, one day my grandmother and the nuns went at it as she insisted that they call me Jay; it went on and on and eventually my grandmother won. She was like that as she was a strong mixture of German and Irish. She was a strong supporter of the Democratic party and was one of the first ladies to run for the legislature in Kentucky. My grandfather was a banker who exercised every day by swimming at the local YMCA. He was not that caring and was a little bit aloof and quiet. He usually didn't yell at us, but when he did, you had better listen. Every summer when we visited, they would sit on the porch and drink beer or bourbon with my Uncle Red. There was always laughter and jokes; however, nothing was ever too serious and it lasted well into the night. On my mother's side, my grandmother was very short in stature and was very strict; there was very little horseplay in her house.

My grandfather was a dentist in the navy and upon discharge opened a dentist office in downtown Cincinnati. They were much more affluent than my dad's side, which had more of a modest means. My grandfather also had antique cars as a hobby. He had a 1910 Ford, a Packard, and a 1931 Ford truck, which were assembled from the frame up. He used to take us for rides in the antique cars, and we were able to wave to the people that looked at the passing car. He had also assembled a jitney, which we used to love taking for rides. After he passed away, I was fortunate enough to be able to purchase the Ford truck, which sits in my garage. I still maintain it and drive it around the area; because of its age, people are always honking their horns and waving or giving me the thumbs-up. We spent our two-week vacation going back and forth between the two houses cutting through the woods to get there.

Moving to Florida in first grade, we still attended Catholic school. I was somehow always in trouble with the nuns. My mother was adamant about sending us to school in jeans when the school had its own dress code, which was cotton dress pants. My mother was tired of buying new pants every time we fell down and ripped our pants. Somehow, they reached a compromise, and we continued to where our uniforms but with jeans.

The girls were always playing jokes on me as I was small in stature. In our school, the bathrooms were down a hall. Left was boys and right was girls. One of their favorite "jokes" was to drag me into the girls' bathroom in which a nun would invariably find me. I spent a lot of time getting punished as you didn't want to go against God.

On another occasion, we waited for our ride to pick us up with Holly and Donna who lived down the street and also attended the school. Their father was late by at least an hour when we decided to start walking home. Well, we didn't live close to home so there was no way we would get anywhere near home. We were found by their father down by a lake that was on the way and really got in trouble for trying to walk home rather than wait. Our parents were extremely mad but at the same time trying to teach us a lesson about being safe. It went right over our heads.

In the fifth grade, we started to go to public school; however, we still had to go to mass every Sunday, say confession, and eat fish every Friday. That part didn't change. I attended the only school in Pinellas County that was attempting a new program that separated a small group of individuals who were moving at a faster academic pace and moved them into a single class. This group remained intact throughout elementary, junior, and senior high school. Math and Science were my strong suits and English grammar my weakest. You had to get at least a B average in all subjects to stay in the program. I had to study really hard to get the grades.

Growing up in Florida was a lot of fun. My brothers and sister spent many years with our neighborhood friends running through orange groves and seeing who could top the other. We spent many days fishing in Lake Seminole, and if not fishing, we would be playing baseball or football or we would be lobbing rotten grapefruits at the cars on ALT 19. We were always trying to see who could best the other. I had two brothers and a sister, Phil, James, and Dawn. We were close in age. My brothers were a year behind each other and then skip a year for my sister. My parents must have been very active, or we just coincided with my father's shore leaves. Phil was more independent while Jamie and I had a lot of the same interests. My sister just tried to be close to each of us.

My mother was always a strict disciplinarian, so if we got into trouble, we could expect a beating with the hairbrush. My father played high school and college football until he blew his knee out and lost his scholarship. He then went into the Navy where he learned electronics and flew aircraft off an aircraft carrier. When he got out of the navy, he worked for himself as a TV repairman. Eventually, he got a job with GE Nuclear Devices in the Tampa Florida area. To him, sports were everything; because of this, I played baseball in the Little League program. I was very mediocre, so they stuck me out in right field and kept me in the hitting rotation because of my height as my strike zone was extremely small, and I got on first base a lot by being walked. On the other hand, fans groaned whenever the ball was hit to right field because I would inherently run in and the ball would go over my head.

We did not live in the most expensive area; the neighborhood was of modest means. I had lots of friends in the neighborhood and my closest friend was Bobby Reed who lived a street over. We were inseparable in grade school and junior high. We spent a lot of time fishing together and watching horror movies on Friday nights. The others were neighborhood friends across the street and the two girls down the street, Donna and Holly. Days were spent going to school, playing sports, fishing, and of course doing our homework. We also hunted a lot for snakes and usually found them. There were water moccasins, rattlesnakes, coral snakes, a whole host of garter snakes and king snakes. We played with the nonpoisonous ones and stayed away from the others. The area was full of orange groves, pastures, and lots of vacant ranch land.

There was always something to do. Behind our house was vacant land covered with cane plants, orange, and grapefruit trees. There was also a small pond that included our two resident alligators. We had developed a lot of trails through the cane fields so that we could travel around without knowledge. We all went to the same schools and rode the same school bus. As we got older, we developed friends outside of the neighborhood. We also pursued other interests in drive in movies, cars, part-time jobs, and girls.

Halloween and Christmas were my favorite times of the year. On Halloween, we used to dress up and get the biggest bag that we could. We would go with our friends and cover an incredible amount of houses in and outside our neighborhood and would fill our bags with candy. This was important for us because we didn't get much candy through the year so we would make our stash last for a while. It wasn't until we were teens that we began pulling pranks on those houses that did not give us candy, usually with a rotten egg or soap. We had a blast on Halloween and the memories last forever.

Christmas was always the best. My mother would save money all year long from her dog grooming and selling puppies. We had one poodle named Irma that would produce litters of seven to eight puppies twice a year. She would then use the money to buy Christmas presents. Whether it was a bike or skateboards, she would always give us the latest fad both in toys and clothes. My dad would sit up most of the night assembling toys. I have fond memories of those Christmases even today. Later in life, we would have Christmas at my Grandma Rose's house which was always a blast as it was the last stop on our day. We would have dinner and then open presents. You would never know what you would get especially from my aunt and uncle. They would wait until the last moment and then go to Value City and buy gifts. They were usually something bizarre that you had no intention of wearing or playing with. But there was plenty of love and laughter, and I really miss those Christmases. One year I flew my girlfriend Alice up from Florida to be with us at Christmas. I had been dating her steady for about the last three years. She had a lot of fun and probably met the most dysfunctional family ever.

Sports in junior and senior high school were a nightmare for me. At five feet, six inches and a whopping ninety-eight pounds, I was the brunt of all the jokes. After we completed our laps of running around the field, the coach would always say, "Is Braukman still here?" I don't want to lose him down an ant hole. Fortunately, I was smart so I could trade academic help for a little protection but every day in the locker room was a nightmare because of the practical jokes like hanging me from the coat hook by my underwear. Some of the jokes just became cruel, and I was always late for my next class.

Sports meant a lot for my father so in high school, I ran cross-country to get my school letter. I usually finished fifth on the team, but it was enough to keep us in the total placement (as a team) in the event. I also wrestled in the ninety-eight-pound weight class as another activity and was pretty good. On one cross-country race, my coach dropped me down to junior varsity so that I could maybe win. Unfortunately, I had been drinking the night before and I started out much too fast. I was running in first place and held that position for at least half the race, but then the effects of not pacing myself and the previous night took effect, and I wound up puking my way to the finish line nowhere near first place My dad was proud that I lettered. He was also proud that he could brag about my academic skills as well as being elected class president for my sophomore and junior years (I should note that high school was only three years at that time).

Instead of going for a third year as class president (which had never been accomplished), instead, I tried to win student council president rather than senior class president and lost because I failed to get the sophomore vote (this would have been the new class coming over from junior high). This group of individuals just did not know me personally; I did not spend enough time courting this group of voters as I felt they would follow their upper classmates' advice. This was not the case and my opponent who courted this vote heavily won this group of votes and with the straggler of votes in junior and senior class won the election. I was devastated; I had never lost before and felt embarrassed to walk the hallways. Privately, I determined that I would not make that mistake again. After the election, the administration tried to find an office for me to have because they wanted me involved in high school leadership. I joined a lot of extracurricular organizations and was always involved with school activities whether it be yearbook, homecoming, young republicans, fund raising events or the class prom. At the end of the day, I was always doing a lot and was proud of what I accomplished.

In between my junior and senior years, there was a unique program supported by the local organization in which top individuals were selected to attend Boy's State. This was a program where the states "best" went to Tallahassee (Florida State University). We played a mock version of our form of government structure (democracy), which included the legislature (house and senate), judicial and executive branches. We decided what office we would attempt to be elected to and then perform sessions and speeches to give you a feeling of what the process was all about (selection of office and the election). I was elected to congress, and following this, we met in groups to develop the laws and proposals that would be beneficial to future school years. I focused on changing the dress code (this was the late sixties, early seventies, and being able to wear jeans and long hair were important). We developed a law, introduced it to be voted on, and sent it to the senate.

LESSONS OF EXPERIENCE

It was then that the real legislation could pick up the bill and develop it as a real bill to the house. We had essentially started a change in the dress code of the Florida school system. After attending, you returned to your city and gave a presentation to the local organization, school principals, county reps, etc. I hated public speaking, but the exposure you received was incredible.

It was at this time that I was preparing to take the test to get my learners permit to drive. My mother had taken me to get the test, and as I was signing in, the officer asked me what my mother's maiden name was. I responded "Hewetson" as this is what I had always known. My mother then corrected me and said her maiden name was "Waltman." I sat there thinking, "Who the hell is Waltman?" She said that we could talk about it after I took the test. I passed my test (small wonder with what had just happened), and we went out to lunch. She proceeded to tell me that my real grandfather was some man named Waltman and that the family had kept it quiet for all these years and didn't want anybody to know that my grandmother had a previous husband. I had a lot of questions; some were answered others were not.

Later that day, I thought about all the summers that I had spent with my grandfather (that I knew). The rides on the Go-karts, the trips to Coney Island, the annual dentist checkup and filling of cavities (he was a dentist in downtown Cincinnati), and all the memorable times we had together. He had given me unrequited love for all these years and had treated me as he would any other grandchild. I decided that it didn't matter that he wasn't my blood grandfather because he was the grandfather that had loved me all these years. I never really learned anything about my blood grandfather other than he had died of a heart attack in his fifties.

I never met the man and nobody would give me any information for me to even try. It's funny, because I had always thought I was almost pure German because of our last name of "Von Braukmann." My great-grandfather dropped the Von and my grandfather dropped one of the Ns, shortening it to "Braukman." Recently, I sent my DNA off to get tested and it turns out that I am over 60 percent from England, Scotland, and Ireland. What a surprise!

During my junior year, my dad had bought a new yellow 1964 Ford Mustang. It was a three-speed and was awesome. He only had carpool duty for one week out of the month so I could use it for three weeks out of the month. This solved my problem of needing rides for all my extra-curricular activities. It also gave me a neat car to date with or just cruise the local drive through on weekends. I loved that car. It was only a six-cylinder engine so that the only way you could burn rubber was in reverse. My father was always wondering how I kept dropping transmissions and using up the back tires. I obviously never told him.

After school for my junior and senior years, I work for a grocery store as a bagger, stock boy, and other various jobs, including unloading the trucks as they came in. We used to hide a case of beer or a bottle of wine behind the crates and pallets and pick it up later that night. We always had parties on the weekends. Some on the beach and others at friends' homes.

There was usually some drinking, and this was also the age of experimenting with pot and acid. One double date, we had gone to the drive-end movies. We had a six pack of beer and were getting into some kissing and petting. One of the beers had fallen down between the seats, and when I pushed back the seat to get the beer, it was punctured and spilled all over the floor. We tried to clean it up and used some perfume to hide the smell. The next morning, my dad got into the car, and when he returned home, he asked me why it smelled like a French whorehouse. All I could say was that my date had spilled some perfume. (He never asked why my date was in the backseat.)

Right before my senior year, my father was transferred to Cincinnati, Ohio. I really didn't want to move for my senior year. My parents were sympathetic to my situation given the amount of activities that I was involved in. They arranged for me to stay in Florida with some close friends of theirs. He owned a gas station and made a living pumping gas and being a mechanic. She raised show dogs as did my parents. They were really nice people whose children were already out of the house. I bought an old Triumph convertible to go back and forth to school and work. It burned more oil than gas, and every time you took off from an intersection, you left a plume of smoke.

Also, the trunk lid was not attached to the body so every time you turned a corner sharply, the trunk lid would slide off into the intersection and you would have to retrieve it. It was very embarrassing, but it was all I could afford. I must have kept them crazy keeping late hours. I wouldn't get off from work until nine thirty, and on weekends, I stayed out very late usually partying or just cruising. I had a friend at work who owned a small Kawasaki motorcycle. I used to trade him my car to ride his bike. Usually, I went over and picked up this really cute redhead and would just go for a ride. She really liked to ride on the motorcycle. I think it just erotically aroused her. We had fun though, and besides the rides, I dated her a couple of times.

On one occasion, we started out in the morning and rented a fishing boat. We went out past the US coastline and drank beer and fished all day long. When we came in, we decided to go to a party. It was at someone's house that I didn't know but he seemed okay. He started giving us hard alcohol to drink, and the next thing I remember was waking up with cuts and bruises all over my body. I couldn't understand what happened or how I got home let alone in bed. I started questioning my friends and no one wanted to tell me what happened. Finally, someone told me that I was really drunk and had fallen off a three-story building into some bushes on the beach, which broke my fall. They then proceeded dropping me off on the doorstep of Carl and Helen's house. I never knew how I wound up in bed, but I never asked and they never said anything. We celebrated our senior year by having senior skip day at a local quarry. We were drinking beer and having a lot of fun when I asked to borrow my friends' Indian motorcycle. I drove it up and down this dirt road to the quarry and was increasing my speed. All of a sudden, I hit a pothole and the front wheel turned sideways. The bike proceeded to flip over and over luckily not hitting me but I slid for a long distance on the road and really tore up my body with abrasions. The mask on the helmet I was wearing had a big hole in the plastic face shield from the sliding. The bike was in pieces and was a total loss. Someone called the police, and he came and investigated the incident.

I told him that somebody had driven me off the side of the road. He issued me a ticket for not having the bike inspected. We took the bike home in pieces in the back of someone's truck. His father was really pissed but was also very concerned about the liability of not having the bike properly inspected. I wound up giving him my car for the bike as I was leaving to go north in a month. I hid the abrasions by wearing a long-sleeve shirts and long pants. I was lucky to be alive.

My best friend during my senior year was a guy named Tim. He owned a really neat Ford Galaxy. We went everywhere with it, including picking me up and driving me to school so that I didn't have to take the Triumph. Usually we were hanging out at the local McDonald's until we came across a party then off we went. We double-dated a lot as I didn't want to take any date in my car. One night, we were just driving around and wound up trying to take a shortcut. Well, we didn't see any stop sign and blew through a dead end. The car went into a large drainage ditch and wound up on its side.

After seeing that we were both okay, we crawled out the driver-side window. The accident had made a hell of a lot of noise and the adjoining neighbor had come out to see what happened. He immediately called the sheriffs' department, and we soon had company. After investigating the accident, he didn't issue any citation as the intersection was not marked. We had the car towed and Tim's parents were really pissed off about the damage.

He was grounded for a couple of weeks. We were always trying to figure what trouble we could get into and one morning on the way to school we decided to share a bottle of Boone's Farm wine. We arrived at school pretty well drunk and made in through homeroom. During the first period, our teacher was somewhat sympathetic and told us to put our heads down on the desk and stay quiet. That wasn't hard to do. By lunch, we were pretty well sober and made it through the day. The only real disagreements that we had were when we liked the same woman. We would really get competitive fast to see who could date her first. We were also in all the same classes and had the same extracurricular activities, so it made it easy to travel to and from school. We always had something to do after school; however, he was not an athlete, so I wound up practicing and going to track meets on my own.

A couple of years after graduation, I found out that he had become a pretty big local DJ. I did, however, keep tabs on Bobby as he had become close friends with my brother Jim (as he wants to be called now). They spent a lot of time fishing together. He went on to become the produce manager for a local Publix supermarket.

During my sophomore, junior and beginning of my senior year, I dated a woman named Alice. She was in all my classes, and we were inseparable; we did everything together. The only time we were apart was when I was elected homecoming king and spent the time with the homecoming queen. My parents really liked her, so she spent a lot of the time with our family. It was only natural, spending so much time together, that we would begin exploring each other's bodies. We would lie outside in her backyard on a lounge chair and usually began some heavy petting. I usually took care of her and I went home aching in my private areas. I often wondered what her parents thought we were doing in the backyard at night. One time, there was nobody in her house and we went into her bedroom and began taking off our clothes. I thought we were going to finally do more, when unexpectedly, her sister opens up the front door. We scrambled to get dressed and then came out. She started to grill us on what we were doing, and of course, we said nothing happened, which was true.

Women in our class were inseparable as they all took the same classes and shared all the same secrets. It truly was impossible to do anything that everyone in the class would immediately know about it. Alice had gone to the movies with her girlfriends and there was a part in the movie where another woman asks the star what she had been doing for the summer, and she states "growing a penis." Well, Alice could not tell me about the movie as she said she would be too embarrassed. Her friend eventually told me. I couldn't go see the movie because it was rated "R," and I was not old enough to see it (Alice was a year older than I was). We had a considerable amount of fun times together, and we truly cared for each other. She had gone to Idaho in between my junior and senior year to visit relatives and friends. It felt like she was gone for a year. However, we knew that we were both going off to different universities, so during our senior year, I decided to break up with her so that I could date other women.

There were plenty of parties to attend on the beach. I was also able to date other women that I had a crush on. She was devastated and made me feel really guilty. Everyone tried to get us back together. Our break up was one of the biggest events, and everyone knew about it, including all the teachers. But we didn't get back together; although we obviously still cared a lot for each other and remained friends. In our senior year yearbook, she had a picture taken off her in a teddy with the caption of "Baby, I need your lovin'." To this day, I often wonder what happened to Alice as she was my first "true love".

Usually, after a date, you were lucky if you got a goodnight kiss, but there were others that you could get further along with.

There was one woman that I asked for a date; we spent the night at the drive-through and a movie. On the way home, we parked in a vacant area and started kissing. The next thing I know is she removed her top and had the most beautiful breasts and then proceeded to pull down her pants. I was in shock and kind of didn't know what to do next. I had never encountered a woman that was that forward and wasn't prepared to go that far and certainly didn't want to get her pregnant. I told her it wasn't a good idea, and she got pissed because she thought I felt she was too forward and was embarrassed. We ended that evening, but it was the last date between us. She started dating a guy on the football team, and I'm sure he didn't have the same issue that I had. After that, I was always a good Boy Scout and followed the motto of "Be prepared."

It was here that I met Sue from the swim team. We went to the senior prom and the senior skip school day held at the local reservoir, and I spent my last moments in high school dating her and having fun. She also taught me a little more about sex that was mutually pleasurable without going all the way. We both knew it wasn't a long-term relationship so we made the most of it while we had time.

Looking back, we were probably not that different from any other generations. Toward the end of my senior year, I was focused on two things, getting into the US Coast Guard Academy and Sue from the swim team.

We were some of the most highly recruited individuals for college. The academics were easy and way beyond the rest of the graduating class. I went to school, practiced for cross-country and wrestling, went to work at the supermarket, and partied. Unfortunately, a friend and I had got into trouble for vandalism in my junior year. There were two others in the car, but we had dropped them off before we got pulled over. We were taken to our parents' homes. I had to sit in the back of the sheriff's car while he talked to my friends' parents, and then we went to my house. Imagine waking your father up at 2:00 AM telling him that a Pinellas County sheriff wanted to talk to him. My father listened to what we had done, and it was absolute quiet. My dad just turned to me and said, "We will talk about this tomorrow."

I laid awake for the rest of the night, and as it turned out, the punishment was not extreme from a physical standpoint but his silence and demonstrated disappointment hurt more than anything else. In the meantime, the pricks at the Pinellas County Sheriff's Department made sure the whole school knew about it. The next Monday, they dragged us out of our classes and to the principal's office so they could display their big "bust." Because of this event and the fact that we had become "rebellious" during our senior year, the principal decided that we were not permitted to sit on stage at our graduation with the honor society and other dignitaries of the class.

So the fact that I had achieved more from an academic basis, played sports, and other outside school contributions than anyone that graduated, I was not able to sit with our peers on stage. Over the years, despite the fact that we were together for almost seven years, we tried to keep track of everyone; however, upon graduation, we each went our separate ways.

In retrospect, we didn't know it at the time but what we were doing was networking. Rather it be the Lion's Club, young Republican's, Rotary Club, principal, state senators, teachers, other parents, work or with each other, we were building resumes to benefit us going forward. In addition to grades, universities want to see not only high grade-point averages but also extracurricular activities to see that you did something more than just attend school.

The grades and activities are preparing you for the future and giving you a network of supporters. At the end of the day, it is you that will generate the effort of being the best. You should make the most out of your high school years as this is the time when you begin to think about what you will do with your life. At graduation, you may still not know what you want to do. Many individuals still do not know what they want to do, but have the ideas of what they'd like to do. Choose your college major carefully with the thought that if you change majors, the credits earned can be used toward your new major without having to repeat courses. Maintain your network of supporters so they can give you advice going forward.

CHAPTER 2

The College Years

As soon as I arrived in Cincinnati in 1971, my brothers had arranged a blind date with a girl named Pam. One that they thought was funny as we were completely different people. We joined another couple and went to a drive-in to see *Little Big Man*. The couple we were with fought the entire movie and all the way back home. It was just a little overwhelming, and we agreed that we would go out next week by ourselves. There was one group of individuals in town, and we continued to go out with them frequently that summer. We were all dressed in bellbottom jeans and were doing our best to be hippies spending a lot of time just listening to music.

Pam and I continued to date pretty steady for the rest of that summer before I started college in the fall. In October, I was invited by several of the women that I went to high school with to come up to Antioch College to visit them for the weekend. Somehow, Pam found out that I was going and we had a big fight. She insisted that she come along, which was a disaster. Upon arrival, it was clearly evident that the women had planned for me to be alone. I probably missed out on a great weekend with the women as it became awkward, to say the least, with Pam in tow.

Both of our families owned a house on Coldwater Lake near the southern border of Michigan. Pam's uncle was on one end, and my aunt on the other side. The odds of this happening were extremely low. One weekend, Pam's cousin, Terry, and his wife set up a party at the lake along with her older cousin Victor. Later in the afternoon, Victor's wife showed up as she thought he was seeing someone else. A big fight ensued, and he got in his car and left. She took another car and kept ramming it into Victor's car.

As a result, both cars were trashed. The police arrived shortly after, and both of them went to jail. In the evening, the party was still going strong, except me, I was grumpy and tired. There was a lot of drinking and smoking pot and Terry approach me and said that if I didn't take her to bed tonight then there were plenty of friends who would. I had been dating her through the summer, and deep down, I was pretty sure she wouldn't do that but now I was completely pissed off and I wondered how many times that this had happened before, so I took a boat and parked it in the middle of the lake.

It was just me and a couple of beers. I eventually calm down enough to go back. Pam had wondered where I had gone, so we laid down in one of the beds and just talked it through. We eventually went to sleep, and the next morning, we cleaned up and headed back to Cincinnati. We would go back to Bloomington, Indiana, and to the lake as often as we could. A few years later, her cousin and his wife got a divorce; later we found out that he was gay. In the spring and summer, the homes were always occupied one way or the other as it was only a three and a half-hour drive.

I went to the University of Cincinnati, as that was where GE transferred my father to work. He had gotten a promotion to a manager of a GE service shop, which repaired mostly large motors. He just could not afford college tuition with room and board plus living expense so we worked and paid our own way through college commuting every day up and down the interstate. It was a forty-five-minute drive unless it snowed or rained and then it could be an hour and you prayed that there wasn't an accident as that really screwed up the commute. Not being on campus doesn't allow you to participate in extracurriculum activities. No football, basketball games, extra curriculum activities, or parties.

Because of the Vietnam War, I enlisted in the Reserve Officer's Training Corp (ROTC). The group of individuals that were in ROTC could not be drafted. The deferral from being drafted was for two years while you completed basic military leadership courses. You had to wear your uniform on campus every week on "Parade days" (despite being spit on, verbal abuse, and sometimes some pushing and shoving). In between the freshman and sophomore years, we went out for military maneuvers for a week.

This is where you would learn military tactics and play war with spotters who would call you dead when you screwed up. After two years, you had to commit for your remaining two years of college (which the military would pay for) and commit to an assignment of four years in the service. However, the army could not guarantee that I would be able to join their adjunct generals program. Most likely, I would be sent to Vietnam as a second lieutenant. As a result of not being able to become a lawyer, I dropped out of ROTC and would take my chances with the draft. I had a very low number (103) so I was sure I would be drafted. I received my preliminary notification of drafting, just at the time that the war was ending, and as a result, all draft notices were cancelled. I then, no doubt, could complete my junior and senior year without the possibility of being drafted. My gamble to drop out of ROTC was a good decision as it kept me from a serving four years in a field that was not what I wanted to do with my career.

I initially wasn't a very good student; I spent a lot of time playing cards in the rec room, and as a result, not studying as much as I should have. I felt that I could just attend the classes and that I would be okay. Boy was I wrong and my first semester grades were a nightmare. I had some problems with some of the classes, in particular, my German and English classes. In the first two classes in German, I was able to get a C, which wasn't a disaster but certainly pulled my GPA down.

However, when I got to the third semester, it was German writing. I just could not learn the proper grammar and structure to form a sentence. Some people are good in these types of classes but my strengths lied in Math and Sciences. My professor was sympathetic to my situation, and we agreed that if I never took another class in German then she would give me a D, and I would complete my language requirements. She had nothing to worry about as I had no desire after this experience to learn the language.

The other class was freshman English. These classes were definitely cut courses used to weed out the lower-grade individuals and you had to take them. In the first semester, the professor would give you an assignment and you were required to write about a classic book. Not only did you have to read the book, but you had to write a long paper about the book. English grammar was a problem by its self, but add to it the content of the paper, and I just kept getting lower grades. Pam would correct some of the grammar, but it didn't help as I continued to get mediocre grades. I took the very easy way out by dropping the class, and I would pick it up later. The second English class was in poetry, and I just didn't like the course. Reading poetry and writing what the author was supposedly thinking drove me nuts.

Who knew what the author was thinking! Certainly I didn't after 150 years. One day, the professor asked me what I thought of poetry, and I responded that I thought all poets were queer. He strongly advised me to drop the course because there was no way that I was going to pass. Another class I would have to repeat.

In my sophomore year, we had a professor that refused to conform to the classic way of teaching and grading. He would come to class looking as a sixties hippie. He explained that we would have a midterm and final, but the grades didn't matter because all you had to say was I attended classes, and I learned a lot. You would then give yourself an A. I loved this class and believe it or not I did attend the classes as I was curious of what he would teach.

I spent my freshman and sophomore years taking all the required courses in math, science, English, history, language, and psychology. My last two years were heavily weighted toward my major in accounting in which I got As and Bs, but I was putting in a lot of studying.

At the beginning of my junior year, my father purchased a three-floor apartment right down the street from the university; it was a real blessing and worked out financially as he had three children attending UC. However, despite being a couple of blocks from the university, there was still no time for many extracurricular activities as between full-time classes and work, there wasn't much free time.

There was myself and two brothers that could use the apartments. We rented out the first floor to a husband and wife who were associate professors. I lived on the second floor by myself and later with Pam and my brothers and one of their friends took the third floor. It was a great solution to the housing and commute issue. My father charged us very low rents and this money along with the first-floor rent paid for the monthly mortgage. Also, when we were all graduated, he could sell the building for a profit. The downside was I had to live with my brother Phil. He lived on the third floor. I don't think there was a day that he wasn't drinking or taking something funky. On one of my many visits to his apartment (to ask him to turn down the music), there was a woman stark naked on top of the bedroom sheets.

She wasn't shy and loved to turn people on, myself included (we worked at the movie theater together and she was always flirting). My brother would be arriving shortly so I said goodbye and went downstairs. My brother was one of those people who did not have to study. Grades were easy for him. He carried an A- GPA with little or no effort. However, he dropped out with a couple of quarters left to start his own computer company. That was the very compulsive person that he was. He used to really bug me because he thought I was a geek because I liked to watch *Little House on the Prairie* and the Waltons, and because I wouldn't party all the time. One time, I walked up one night and found him passed out on the sofa with his friends still partying. His head was on top of the wooden armrest.

I started picking up his head and dropping it on armchair (not hard). He woke up the next day wondering why he had such a bad headache. One of our largest issues was food as we never had money. We would go down to the market every weekend and try to get enough food to last a week. One of our main staple was macaroni with tomatoes. It wasn't exactly healthy, but it made due. One time when I was sleeping with Pam, he came into the bedroom and said that we should enjoy our last night on earth as he was going to kill us in our sleep. He really did have a problem. I never liked to be around him when he was drinking or taking something because instead of being happy, he became just another mean drunk which explains why we were never very close.

He ruined a lot of family get-togethers with his drinking. My other brother graduated and moved back to Florida to eventually be a COO of a ship repair company. My sister graduated from high school and went to technical school to become a Chef.

During my sophomore year, I worked as an usher at a local movie theater. It only had one screen and was not that large. It mainly showed movies after they had run at large-chain movie theaters. I basically walked through the theater during the movie, making sure no one was smoking or being disruptive. I also sold refreshments and popcorn at the concession stand. My assistant was the woman that I mentioned previously. She was a divorcee and had one child. She was also looking for a new husband and anybody that looked successful was a candidate. Flirting, dating, and alluring men into bed were her mode of operation. We also ran classic movies. One of the customer's favorites was the running of Reefer Madness.

They went wild for this one week run and attended it like a religion. Trying to stop them from smoking pot during this movie was impossible and you got high just walking up and down the aisle. It was pandemonium for a week. We also ran The Little House of Horrors, another fan favorite. The place was owned by a homosexual man who spent the day and night up in his office doing God knows what. I managed to stay a distance from him as he was just weird. It wasn't much of a job, but it was some money. I kept this job until early into my junior year.

I also tried to deliver newspapers on the weekend. It required getting up at 3:00 AM and wrapping the newspaper and then going on the route throwing newspapers to the subscribers so you had to memorize which house got a paper. I managed to get pulled over by the police one night, asking me if I knew I was driving down the wrong side of the road. It was a lousy job that screwed up your weekends so it only lasted for about three months.

During the summer months, a local company (Nu-Maid Margarine) had a summer program to hire college students to work on their production lines. My uncle worked for the company, so I was able to get hired. The job was extremely boring, either putting bowls on the line to be filled, working the lids, or packing cases. We would change jobs periodically to cut down on the boredom. It was here that I met John. He was a good Catholic boy with a great sense of humor.

We would work the line together and on break talked about or experiences in our college classes as we both were attending UC. After work, we would stop by a local tavern and drink beer and joke around. John was dating a really pretty girl (also a Catholic). We would get together (Pam and me) and play cards or some other activity. They seemed like the perfect couple. We spent so much time with them that he eventually became my best friend and then my best man at my wedding. They were the perfect couple. Her father owned a nursery, which was always nice to visit and look at all the plants. They eventually got married, and I thought their marriage would last forever; however, six months later, Carol had cheated on John with a guy from the race track. It seemed hard to believe. They got separated and later were able to reconcile, which made everyone happy.

LESSONS OF EXPERIENCE

Pam's parents were really nice people and her mother was a saint. We would spend most weekends at her parents' home grilling steaks and fixing a salad. The next-door couple also came over. It was fun as they were always in a good mood. After dinner, we would play cards until around midnight. I always wanted to win, and I enjoyed the company as I didn't have that many friends at college. The next-door neighbors had two boys, we always thought that the older son (a teenage boy) was always looking into the living room to watch what we did after everyone went to sleep. I'm sure he got a lot of education.

Unfortunately, he failed to make a curve in downtown Cincinnati one weekend night because his speed was just too much, and he slammed into a concrete wall, he was killed instantly along with all his friends in the car. His parents were devastated and were not the same after the accident. It was a tragedy all the way around. I couldn't imagine their grief and could only hope that with time it would be less painful.

Through all this, Pam informed me the summer before my senior year that her parents were moving to Michigan because of a job transfer and that if we wanted to stay together we would have to get married. (In retrospect, I do not know why we had to get married rather than just live together.) My parents were very unhappy that I made the decision to get married, as they were concerned that I would not complete my education. In the State of Ohio, you had to be twenty-one or have your parents' approval. They did not agree with my decision but signed for me anyway. Fortunately, just before my senior year, I was informed that I had received a grant, a scholarship, and a student loan, which gave me enough money for my tuition and books. I was also lucky that I found a job working nights at the children's hospital. My duties were to file all the charts left over from the day shift, send up any charts that were requested by the emergency room, and attempting to locate misplaced files.

It was a manual system with each chart being given a six-digit number. It turned out that I was very good at figuring out how individuals could misplace files. They would usually reverse a combination of the first three or last three numbers. Generally, trying different combinations of these numbers would locate the chart. It was a great job as I completed the work in about two to three hours. One of the great perks of the job was that I could eat free at the hospital's cafeteria and then spend the time that was left studying for my next day's college assignments; it was a great arrangement.

In my last semester, I was faced with the prospect of needing twenty-one credit hours in my major (seven courses) to graduate with my class. A normal load of accounting classes would be in the nine- to twelve-hour range. The dean of the college requested that I come to her office as she was very concerned regarding allowing me to take the twenty-one hours of accounting classes, which included accounting theory (a long paper on a chosen topic). I made a deal that if I did not have a B average or better at the midterm that I would drop down to a normal range and graduate in the fall. It wasn't easy and required me to study every spare moment, but I succeeded in getting the grades and graduating with my class in June 1975.

During this time period, the economy was in a terrible recession and jobs were hard or near impossible to find. The accounting firms had come in and took the top five to ten individuals so I wasn't going to get a job with one of the big firms. I read the jobs board every day and took as many interviews as I could. However, nothing ever popped. It was a long summer and fall, and there was no doubt that I was discouraged. I wondered if I would ever find a job in finance. Thank God that I still had my job at the hospital.

CHAPTER 3

Joining GE

A friend suggested that I interview with GE at their local sales office. I had not done this because for whatever reason, I did not want to work for the same company as my father. I took the interview anyway and the summary of that interview and recommendation along with my resume went to Medical Systems in Milwaukee, Wisconsin. At the very same time, Medical Systems was getting corporate criticism for hiring too many University of Wisconsin graduates and were directed to expand their current hiring positions from candidates outside the University of Wisconsin's system.

    I was very surprised on that January evening when I got a call from Medical Systems asking if I wanted to join their business on the Financial Management Program (FMP). I was very familiar with the program and immediately accepted; we determined the start date, salary, and the person to contact when I arrived. I hung up the phone and turned to Pam asking where in the hell Wisconsin was. When I looked on the map, all I could say was "oh shit" as I had a tremendous fear of driving in winter and snow. At the end of the month, we loaded up the car with all our stuff in the trunk and all the plants in the backseat. Somewhere near Chicago, there were many cars scattered all over the interstate. It was black ice, and being from Florida, I never imagined how difficult it could be to drive on ice.

I pulled into the next gas station (driving 5 MPH) and asked how much longer we were going to have to drive on this shit as I was ready to turn around and go back to Cincy. They told me that once I hit the interstate surrounding Chicago it would be much better. We arrived at the hotel in Milwaukee opened the doors and immediately watched our entire assortment of plants die. I mean immediately as if someone threw a switch. It should have been an omen to turn around and start over. I was met the next morning by a person from the business who took me around the office and then to various apartments that were available for rent. I have never encountered such cold! It was a minus fifteen degrees.

I kept asking who lived in this shit. I mean, how could people survive in this weather. I had a very difficult time adjusting to the climate. I would watch the news, and if they said snow, I would stay awake all night worrying about what could happen. It was a very difficult time adjusting to the surrounding environment. I honestly thought every day would be my last day. We found a small one-bedroom apartment, and I began my career. As background, the Financial Management Program (FMP) was the entry path to all financial positions in GE. You had to pass four classes and four rotational assignments in various elements of finance.

During the summers, which were short, I played softball and golfed. I wasn't good in either one; however, my mentor felt I should get to know the other GE people in the leagues. The softball was a very competitive league and the players took it seriously. I remember that we played a double elimination event one weekend. We must have played five or six games. In one game, I had got a single to left field and was on first base. The guy behind me hit a ball to deep center field, which was bobbled and went all the way to the fence. I took off and rounded second and was heading to third when I got the signal to keep going. I rounded third base way too wide and halfway to home I started to lose my balance. I fell short of home plate and proceeded to crawl home. I had just touched home plate when the player behind me touch home plate. I was really embarrassed that I had fallen down.

At the end of this tournament, my arm was like rubber. I just could not throw the ball back to the pitcher. It was embarrassing, but I had to underhand the ball back to the pitcher and it was usually short. We made it through the game, and at least I didn't give up. Golf was another experience. The golf league was after work one night a week. I was terrible at golf as I sliced the ball on every shot. I should have taken lessons but we didn't have the money. Perseverance doesn't count when you continue to make the same mistakes. I almost killed a guy who walked down the right side of the fairway after he hit his shot. He thought he was safe but I sliced the ball so bad that it just barely missed his head. I was shaking for the rest of the round.

During my FMP assignments, my wife worked at a retail store to supplement our income. We were always short on money because rent in relation to starting salaries was extremely expensive. She had a friend that she had met at work. Jeanie was a pretty woman who was from Canada. She would spend some time with both of us especially on holidays. I remember one trip to Chicago to go shopping. We were in a women's clothing store, and she tried on this really see through blouse. She then came out of the dressing room and asked me how I liked it. You could see right through it. Wow, did she have some great breasts, not extremely big but just well-shaped. I think the both of them enjoyed seeing me turned on. It would not be the last time that I saw that blouse.

My first assignment was in accounts receivable, and I had a wonderful older man in charge of the department. I remember him telling me that I would not go very far in GE because I was too honest. On my very first closing, the books were out of alignment by $2.5 million, which everyone in the business searched for. It turned out that I had made an entry backward, which was a very visible career enhancer! The first class and assignment were easy, and I received an excellent review in my job position. The same happened in the second rotation and class.

By this time, we had lost two of the five individuals from the class who failed a course and had to repeat it. This was the kiss of death for your career prospects. The next class was in cost accounting, which happened to be my worse subject; I just did not get it. I just had a mental block on the subject and the carryover effect of my cost accounting class at UC. My professor, after the first exam in cost accounting, told the entire class that there was one individual who would never make it in the accounting field as he had no clue what cost accounting was all about (that really helped my self-confidence). Singling me out like that was embarrassing. I struggled with the class both at UC and with GE and was barely passing. A failure would have meant the end of any real meaningful career. After the final exam, I was sure that I had failed, but by some miracle, I ended up with a grade of 76, just passing. (Somebody had to have given me points for spelling my name right as there was some latitude in interpreting the grading on questions.)

I had made it through and that coupled with another excellent rotational assignment kept me in the race. The last class was auditing, which for whatever reason, I excelled in. Coupling that with my excellent performance review in my assignment in financial planning and analysis, gave me a lot of positive exposure to the chief financial officer. Overall, I graduated with an average grade point average in the classes and an outstanding ratings in my assignments. In addition, I had gained positive support from some very powerful mentors.

CHAPTER 4

Computerized Tomography

After graduation, there was a position in computerized tomography as a financial analyst. At that time, all jobs were rated at a certain "level" to ensure that the individual was qualified to do the job. Most FMPs graduated at the lowest level (seven) position; however, this particular job was a level 10 working for a financial analyst (who was a great mentor and teacher). I was told that I would have little chance of getting this position. After all the interviews had been concluded, I was told that I had been selected for the position (with the level seven pay). Computerized tomography or (CT) was an unbelievable breakthrough in the medical field. Taking pictures of slices of the brain which gave doctors a significant breakthrough in finding problems and being able to provide a more accurate diagnosis. I was fascinated with the technology.

It also was a job with continuous financial reviews. Because of the rapid advancement in technology, the reviews seemed to happen every other week. Early in my position, it was communicated that Jack Welch was coming for a visit and wanted a review of the computerized tomography program. The review encompassed the status of our relationships with the hospitals, the status of our technology, status of our manufacturing capability, and a financial review. On the morning of the review, both of my bosses had become ill and I was the only person left in the department to perform the presentation. I was also dumb enough not to realize the implication of presenting to Jack. Here I was a brand-new hire from FMP doing a level 10 job as a level seven pay. When it came time during the presentation for the financials, I began the presentation and about halfway through Jack looked up and asked who I was.

I told him that I had recently graduated from FMP and wanted to be part of the CT team. I knew the subject matter pretty well and we completed the financial section responding to all of Jack's questions. I was told later that he was impressed and I received a management award for my part in the presentation. It was the first time that I had met Jack Welch but it would not be the last over the next twenty-three years. As we all know, he went on to be the chairman and CEO of GE.

It was during December and everyone was on vacation, the program team came to me an indicated that they needed an approval for an appropriation request to put a CT unit into the back of a modified semi-trailer truck so that it could go to small locations when CT images were needed. I tried to call someone to get approval (anyone) as I did not have the authority to approve spending $1.5 million dollars. Well, the appropriation request (A/R) had to be approved or the production would halt, and it would not be ready for the largest trade show in North America. I reluctantly signed it and the unit was complete by the time of the show. In the meantime, both the CEO and CFO came back to work.

I was immediately called to the CEO's office and told with no uncertain terms that only he could have approved that amount. He wanted to know if I was going to make it a continuous problem in breaking company policy by signing for CEOs and why shouldn't he fire me? I apologized for the stupidity of signing his approval to an expenditure that he had not approved. He told me to get out and never let it happen again. The CFO who had been standing there with me asked me into his office. He asked me, if there was anything that I did not understand. He then told me it was stupid overstepping my authority and to never let it happen again.

Well, two weeks later, the show opens in Chicago and everyone was there including our CEO, CFO, and Jack Welch. Well, the CT unit that was portable and could be moved from city to city via semi-truck was the absolute hit of the show. When they came back to the business, I received my second management award for excellence.

At the same time that I was doing the financial analyst position for CT, the corporate audit staff was onsite to perform their annual review. To explain, the corporate audit staff was an organization of approximately 125 individuals that performed audits of Businesses in the GE portfolio based on their exposure to the company's financial results. They worked in cooperation with our external auditors (KPMG) to complete the annual audit of the companies accounts and records. Their reviews were subsequently scrutinized by what were called "peer reviews," which commented on the quality of the work papers and work performed. KPMG used those audits to supplement their work to hold down overall costs and the time it took to conduct the review.

It was considered an "honor" to be chosen to work for the audit staff as they took only the best of graduating or first-year graduates interested in taking this career path. It was a grueling and very competitive program and recognized as a fast track program for advancement. They not only took financial management graduates but also the graduates of all other GE programs, Manufacturing, HR, and Engineering. In addition to their normal staff, they also were always recruiting for people who were interested to join the audit staff and provided the opportunity to work with them during their audit.

This audit was being conducted by Dennis Carey who wanted me take a look at our physical inventory process and procedures. The same people who had found a way to get me a 76 percent and pass cost accounting where now under review by me. Unfortunately, I found some issues with the way the physical inventory was performed. I shared my findings with Dennis who provided me with an audit plan to review the impact of the discrepancies. My "friends" in Medical Systems cost accounting now viewed me as a threat. I became "persona non gratis" and everyone was told to not talk with me. I continued my review and reported my findings.

Based on the work completed, Dennis strongly supported my acceptance on the Corporate Audit Staff despite my somewhat mediocre grades in the classwork but excellent reviews in my rotational assignments. I also had some very strong support from key individuals in the business. Having sponsors in GE was extremely critical at every step along the way.

CHAPTER 5

The Audit Staff

So I was about to depart Medical Systems and join the Corporate Audit Staff at the same time we learned that my wife was pregnant. Just before we were ready to head out to drive to Schenectady, NY, her doctor had told her that he couldn't find a heartbeat and felt that the baby had died. He indicated that we really were not going to be sure until her next visit which was three to four weeks away. I called the doctor and asked him if he knew what telling that kind of information would do to a person getting ready to move to a new location and was already nervous because there was not a damn thing that anyone could do for the next three weeks so why tell her? He said he felt obligated to give her his opinion. Let us just politely say I disagreed and told him that he lacked empathy and any type of patient skills.

I asked him if it was his wife or daughter would he want the same treatment and communication. It was a very hard drive going from Milwaukee, Wisconsin, to Schenectady, New York, especially knowing that her next ob-gyn appointment wouldn't be for a month. It was extremely hard on both our minds not knowing whether the baby was alive or dead. After three weeks, my wife received her next appointment, and everything with the baby was fine. I could have killed that first doctor. The corporate audit staff still wanted me to be near to my wife so I received a "four month in town" assignment. A one-month review and a three month assignment (audits were normally three months in duration with returns home dependent on how far away you were either weekly, biweekly, three weeks, or a month). In town assignments were coveted by the auditor's because they could see their husbands or wives every night and on weekends.

At this point, I should probably explain how the corporate audit staff worked. There were audit programs for us to use as guidelines. One of the most idiotic measurements but one that was considered a status of "manhood" was to beat the cost of the previous audits of the same business. At the end of the audit, we were given appraisals of how we performed. They covered both technical and inter-personnel skills (good team player, communicates well, great reviews and findings, intelligence, etc.) These appraisals were critical in determining how far you would be promoted on the audit staff.

There were four audit positions beginning with a junior auditor, semi-senior, senior, and an auditor in charge. In addition, four audit administrators split up the various businesses. As a result, if you could not finish two years, your next assignment would not be one that was a significant promotion. Your goal was jumping into higher levels. In other words, the farther you went on the audit staff the better your position would be coming off the audit staff.

An additional element was that your previous appraisals were shared with your next audit manager.

A bad review would only allow you one additional assignment to straighten out the performance issues from the previous audit. It was a flat-out dog-eat-dog situation. You busted your ass to complete your assignments better than the previous auditor and in a shorter amount of time and get an outstanding appraisal. The hardest part was that the junior auditor was always assigned to get cars and living arrangements remembering that the goal was to beat the cost of the previous audit.

Because of my wife's problematic progression with the pregnancy, I was given a number of in town or close assignments. This would allow me to get home in time to be with my wife if something bad happened. I cannot remember the sequence of the assignments, but only to say that I received unusual "treatment" to get the assignments that I did which created resentment from the other auditors. As I remember, my first audit was to review the corporate payroll system which was a one month review, which included a review and summary (for the annual report) of the corporate officer's expense accounts.

I began the review of the payroll system and went through all the basic audit programs regarding the payroll system with some minor "conflict of duties" and un-reconciled accounts, which was a pretty benign review. While looking at the actual computer programs that determined your weekly, biweekly, or monthly paychecks, I got hung up on where the rounding's of pennies where accumulated. After writing a statistical program to determine the answer, it turned out to be a big nothing. I was excited about the assignment of reviewing officer's expense accounts with the expectations that I would do a thorough review (Rambo style) of expenses. I made it my personal goal to highlight how much and in what manner the officers of the company (approximately 125 individuals) were spending money especially given our personal goal of being "cheap."

I quantified everything, some of the items I remembered were staff dinners and lunches, staff meetings while playing golf, offsite staff meetings, and anything else that I felt was excessive. In reviewing the results of my findings, the auditor-in-charge complemented me on my thoroughness but explained that overall, corporate officers had a tremendous amount of leeway regarding expenses that they felt were appropriate. This gave me a completely new perspective on the leeway that was permitted.

So in the early morning around 3:00 AM on October 3, 1979, we were rushing to get to the hospital and I was pulled over for speeding. Once the officer looked into the car he gave us a police escort to the hospital. The delivery was going fine until the baby went into distress; it was so dramatic and quick we literally rushed to the operating room. During that time (late seventies), husbands were generally not allowed into the operating room but they put me on a stool behind my wife's head and allowed me to see what was going on. The C-section was lightning fast, my spouse was fine, but the baby was blue and not breathing right.

The cord had become wrapped around her neck and she would have died from the continual contractions had they not been so quick in their decisions. As it was, she was a meconium baby (which means that in distress the baby swallowed its first stool) and that the next twenty-four hours would be critical. There were three paths (1) she would have some brain damage, (2) she would die overnight, or (3) she would be fine. My parents rushed from Cleveland and upon getting there were told that the baby was much better (cell phones didn't exist) and with that news they were happy grandparents.

Michelle's birth took place during the fourth quarter and assignments had already been given out. I was assigned to be part of a five- to six-person team to audit Silicone Products. I was given the audit programs of both receivables and cost accounting. I was also requested to keep watch on a "young" auditor who had been given an unsatisfactory review on his first audit. He was really distraught as this meant everything to him and he knew that he was going to be placed into a business as soon as possible (less than a year). This would be like having a big black mark next to his name for any future jobs.

From his perspective, everything that he had worked to achieve was over, and he would have to explain this to his family and close friends. The staff never talked about it but you had all type-A personality traits competing to be the best. With all this competitiveness and personal expectations, some individuals took drastic measures (attempted suicide) as a way out. As an old boss once told me, it was a long-term solution to a short-term problem. The staff would make sure that this assignment was meaningful to him and that he received much personal attention and morale boosts.

Another bizarre episode on this audit was that we woke up one morning to find the front-page headlines having the CEO of the business arrested in a "sting" operation to reduce the number of "homosexual" encounters that were occurring at one rest area off the interstate. His contention was that he had used the facility but had forgotten to put his pants back on properly when he left the facility. It also did not help that he was behind the building not in front of it. He explained that he was just checking on all the commotion. The company placed the CEO on special assignment pending him finding a new position outside the company. This audit really demonstrated that the audit reports and findings always needed balancing with the personal effect to "good people" and although competition was good, keep a close eye on your friends for changes in personality.

Following Silicones, I ran a small audit of a business located in Vermont, which primarily made weapons for the US Government (Armament Systems). I would drive home on Fridays and back on Mondays (in the dead of winter). By now, we know how much I loved to drive in snow or how much a loved cold places but here was a place where the trees only lived five months of the year, and it snowed continuously. I was given one junior auditor and a woman who wanted to "try out for the audit staff." Any qualified candidates recommended by the manager of finance of the Business were eligible.

The individual was assigned for a three-month period so that she would experience every situation that the auditors experienced and given a group of audit programs to complete. As noted earlier, this was a fast track program to "kick start" your career because of the exposure that you received and the business leaders who remembered you. In addition, all audit staff members and past members were constantly recruited by external companies as this was recognized as one of the best training and development programs in the world.

It was a government audit so we had to have all the security clearances, which included the FBI asking old neighbors and friends what kind of person I was. Obviously, I received my clearance but with many phone calls from friends and family as to what was going on and why was the FBI investigating me. However, I was not that good following the activities of my junior auditor as he was staying the weekends "in town" to be with someone. I think we can all figure out who that was. Her work was satisfactory and I have to say so was her effort (no jokes intended). Overall, the audit had some issues, which were agreed to be fixed, and the CFO ask me if I would like to join the business.

I said thanks but no thanks as the weather was not conducive to my lifestyle. I have to say that this was one of the more fascinating audits because of the products that were made. At that time, they were developing an ammunition round that would be able to penetrate a Russian tank. Without giving up the technology, they succeeded and we were able to "watch" the demonstrations of performance on the firing range as the tests were completed. The other weapon produced was the mini-gun that fired a 7.62 mm round, which was capable of shooting up to two thousand to six thousand rounds a minute! Think of that, six thousand rounds a minute! Of course it had to be in spurts as if you shot the gun for a full minute, it would melt the gun barrel. They made other products for future technology that were equally fascinating. Watching them blow things up on the testing grounds was fascinating to me.

On my next assignment, I was finally given a review overseas. Usually an auditor did not get an overseas assignment until their second year. Therefore, I would become one of the youngest auditors to go overseas. I was scheduled to go to join up with the team in Bilbao, which was located in Northern Spain. I had failed a routine physical at the time the team was leaving, so it turned out that I had some slight blood in the urine, and once I saw a urologist, he quickly released me and I traveled alone to catch up with the team. The thought of traveling alone and not being able to speak Spanish was worrisome. I was scared shitless. Somehow, I was able to find my flights and get on the right train to Northern Spain. The facilities were nice; however, traveling back and forth was always an issue.

For one, the audit only got two cars and the combination of both vehicles left one person out. This was temporarily fixed by having me ride in the trunk (boot) so we could save money (but we eventually had to get another car). At first, I felt put out but you become ingrained with the task of always trying to beat the cost of the last audit. Northern Spain was having a long-term political issue with a terrorist organization (the Basque Separatists) attacking anything associated with the government of Spain. As long as the terrorists only attacked government people then the locals would give them hiding—food and whatever they needed. I should have known (an intuition) that this audit was going to be a problem when on the first night, I caught my pants on fire getting too close to a space heater which was necessary because it was extremely cold in the offices.

There were increasing "actions" between the government and the terrorists that continued in both intensity and time. A few weeks after our arrival, there became a major operation. Unfortunately, there was only one road to travel between the hotel and business. On this route was a tunnel; it was not a long tunnel, so people traveling behind traffic could see the daylight at the end of the tunnel. A head of us (by about a dozen vehicles) was a large truck carrying a group of soldiers.

On one of the trips, after about two to three weeks at the business, the Basque separatist had set up a perfect ambush. On both sides at the end of the tunnel were the terrorists with machine guns, which as the truck reached the end of the tunnel, they opened up on the truck from both sides with automatic machine guns until all the soldiers were dead. The US did not see such brutality on a daily basis and considering the lasting effects of the Vietnam news coverage, they did not want to, personally; we had to question whether this was an audit that was worth conducting and completing in these conditions. The Basque separatists killed twenty-eight people in the first thirty days of the audit.

LESSONS OF EXPERIENCE

It was customary that the business would start operations around 9:00–10:00 AM. They took lunch around 3:00 PM (which was followed by a mandatory brandy and cigar) and worked into the evening until 7:30 to 8:00 PM. Restaurants did not start serving until around 9:00 to 10:00 PM. Eating before that was considered rude. Talk about screwing you up from a time stand point, getting "client time" was extremely difficult.

On the first night, I decided that I would order something safe, which I thought, was ravioli. My Spanish was slightly off, and I got scrambled eggs and anchovies. Our diet became limited or thrilling depending on your perspective. About three weeks into the audit, our auditor in charge (AIC) arrived after finishing his last audit. Before this, a senior auditor "who felt this should be a work every day of the week audit" had run the audit.

Do not get me wrong, Saturdays, we did our expense accounts and made our fifteen-minute calls home. However, there needed to be some real down time. The AIC decided that Sundays would be a day of field trips, which the senior auditor disagreed with. You could choose either working with him or going with your teammates to some new location. There was a mixed crowd but most of us were there on Sundays to take our "trip." We usually got back late but had some wonderful times and memories on the northern coastline of Spain. There was some fun Sunday trips in which we were given the opportunity to visit and learn about the local culture. In addition, there was a great restaurant, which served a plate of small eels.

To me, this was the best meal in my life. They were like eating worms. The eels were black; however, you could still see their little eyes. It was a real delicacy. After having a review of our status with the audit administrator taking into account the audit, the environment and the terrorists, we decided to move ahead with the audit. About six weeks into the audit, my assistant and translator (local hire) requested/demanded that we would not go this Friday to the bar that we always went to on Friday nights. Discussing back and forth on why she felt that way, she was adamant to get us to promise that we would not be there. We relayed the story to the rest of the team and decided to try someplace new that Friday night. It was good that we listened because the bar blew up.

I do not know if they would have called it off if we were there but I doubt if five Americans meant much to them in the totality. I should note that it was GE's policy not to negotiate with terrorists, so you always knew you were on your own. You could understand this position, given the amount of US employees' around the world at any point in time. Shortly after the bar blast, I was requested to do an audit of a field office in the town square. It was on the second day that there was a large blast. After picking myself up off the floor and dusting off, I looked out the second-floor window to see a car, which had just exploded. Again, another brutal message sent to the government. They would continue to send their messages and operate from the area of the northern Spanish coast and the French mountain border.

And as before, as long as the brutality only impacted government employees, the locals would continue to give them protection, food, and clothing. The audit was a long three months with trips home only twice. By the time you got home on Friday and had to leave on Monday, the time home was about the same time it took to travel. On a lighter note, we were always playing pranks on each other. Little things such as having your mattress thrown out the window, putting woman's underwear in a friend's luggage home so that his wife would see them when she unloaded the suitcase.

One night, the AIC knocked on my door. When I answered, he was standing there in his underwear asking me if I had some shoe polish. I said no and he went on to the next auditor. At the end of the audit, we said goodbye to the people and "assistants" that helped us (with some special goodbyes to our "translators") and left the region. We each had our own thoughts about the Basque separatists and the acceptance of the people to allow them to operate freely and assist them as long as the fight was between the separatists and the government. As we drove away to catch the overnight train to Madrid, we were all lost in our thoughts and looking forward to seeing family.

Returning home, I was given an unusual audit of a GE business, we owned a small cable TV and radio station in Schenectady, NY. It was a small audit (three to four people) with me in charge. I just wanted to meet the DJs, which operated out of a large broadcasting booth with a large red sign, which when lit read "on air" to let everyone know that the "mikes" were live. The business located us in a small conference room across from the broadcasting booth, and we were going through the normal audit sequences.

Halfway through the audit, one of my auditors came in and stated that he was going to "make history" by proving that the DJs ran new record releases in exchange for taking money and drugs. I patiently listened as he went through his audit plan (on how he was going to "nail them") on this practice. In having discussions and asking questions, it became immediately obvious that he was out of his mind. Well, anyone who knew me had known what would come next, which was "are you out of your "fucking" mind!

As it came out of my mouth, I looked past our open door to see the "on air" sign lit and their door open. I apologized later to the DJs. I shut our door and tried to convince the auditor how stupid his plan was and that he should rethink of how this did not fit into his audit program or scope of review and to let it drop. I knew that I was going to have to explain the series of steps that allowed my comments during an open mike session on air to the listeners (which later, we found out that it was background noise to the speaking DJs). Now it just seems funny, but I can ensure you that I did not find it funny then.

I received a lot of personal coaching on staff and at an audit in Nashville, Tennessee, both the senior auditor and the auditor in charge took me under their wings to make me more presentable as a finance leader. Since graduation from high school, I smoked a pipe, it was a calming effect to a hectic situation, in addition, my office was stacked with business documents for review and it was a mess. I was coached to lose the pipe as a made me looked too academic. It is not easy to quit cold Turkey from any tobacco products. Then one evening, the team was working late to catch up. But I was neck deep in audit paper. The AIC and the senior auditor came into my office and commented on my mess. I told them it was controlled chaos. The AIC looked at my desk and asked if these were current audits. I indicated yes and he said you can only work on one thing at a time and the rest should be in your desk drawers He then announced to the rest of the team that none of us were going home until my office was cleaned up. Everybody loved that one, but I did get my office cleaned up.

The last advice I was given was to lose the frumpy clothes. They indicated that I would become a better leader if I projected a better image. They took me across the street to a mall where I bought several shirts and ties and a blazer to look more professional. That was the extent of the three months audit, and I received a lot of constructive criticism both personally and professionally. I also learned from this experience that whoever you were giving "constructive criticism" too had to be receptive otherwise it would just fall on deaf ears. I readily accepted any advice that was given.

One of the largest businesses in the Schenectady area was the Power Systems Business, which had multiple divisions. One of the largest was the Gas Turbine Business, which would be my next audit. The fact it was an in town assignment was good after monthly visits home from Spain. I should clarify that even when we stayed in town on an audit, it still meant that we would work to 9:00 to 10:00 PM at night but we would be home in our own beds and weekends. It was a large audit team because of the size of the business. I remember the AIC was a female called Teresa. This audit had a history of being extremely contentious between management and the audit staff. We knew going in that this was going to be a difficult audit (for that reason) and that we would try to keep it as civil as we could.

I had the assignment of auditing my least favorite area, cost accounting. At first, the business was very polite and walked me through the entire cost accounting area, and how it fit into the overall finance operation. The business leader was a very nice gentleman who tried to assist me in any effort that I needed. We went back and forth with my requests on explanations of journal entries and I started looking at the physical inventory. It had been conducted using sequentially numbered cards that were then manually counted with the number of pieces found multiplied by its value. In reviewing the sequence of cards, I ran across some cards that just did not make sense (and were not included in the overall valuation). I found this anomaly late at night and on the next day began questioning the individuals.

I was told that they were extremely busy and that I would have to come back tomorrow with my questions. The next day, it became obvious that I was being given the run around and any additional information would have to come from the manager operating the organization. Well, at that point, the nice person quickly became a raving lunatic. His claims were that I had gone through an individual's desk and that I only found out about the cards by stealing them and other documents. He was adamant that I was a thief and lacked integrity. He demanded that I be removed from the audit and be dismissed from the audit staff. (This was some serious shit). The audit that we tried so hard to keep cordial and without incident quickly become a significant issue with tremendous exposure. I mean the man was apoplectic. It went through the ranks like a jet plane coming off an aircraft carrier.

I went through what happened with my auditor in charge and the steps I took to get there. In no way did I break into any desks or file cabinets in the cloak of night. I was asked to do other parts of the audit while this could be resolved. After thinking about it overnight, I became angrier as I had done nothing wrong and this highly ranked manager was calling me a liar who lacked integrity. Because it had gotten so much attention, a review team quickly assembled the facts for management review (I had done nothing wrong). It was resolved, that he would do his job like a professional and allow access to any documents that I requested along with explanations if need be.

I gave it the next couple of days for all to cool down. Following that cooling down time, I was reviewing other journal entries that had been made through the cost accounting journal entries (affecting reserves). I traced an entry, which was for a sizable amount of money. This entry (for the same exact amount) was transferred between different account numbers over the past twelve months. To me, the purpose of this entry was to merely hide some net income so that when they were short they could tap this amount. I returned to the cost accounting area where I met with the same manager that had the previously blown up. I began asking questions, and his response was that cost accounting lessons were closed. I would have to come up with the "right" questions before getting an answer.

This created an even greater resolve for me to ensure that I got to the basis of the entry. In my opinion, this manager was just a complete ass. The audit was winding down and I needed to write the audit findings for these two issues. I kept being grilled on the "mystery" entry that moved the same amount of income from account to account. The AIC ask me if I was sure that this was a kitty. The day before we were going to the Group CFO, the AIC was not comfortable with asking him questions about the entry, especially if this was indeed a kitty to produce net income as needed.

She informed me that I would be going to the meeting with her to explain my findings. The next day, we met with the CFO, and when it was time to explain my audit findings, I asked him what the nature of this account was as it was always the same exact amount that was just moved between various accounts. His response was that it was in fact a kitty and that "he needed it for a rainy day and the raining day was now." He needed the net income so he had no problem with unwinding the entry now. I thought the auditor in charge would fall out of her chair, and quite frankly, I was surprised by his candor. We wrapped up our audit and began to prepare for our next assignments. I was happy that this one was over and that all was resolved regarding the physical inventory. He was forced to apologize that I was not a thief and he had no basis to question my integrity. The apology was good enough for me.

LESSONS OF EXPERIENCE

The most difficult audit for me was a business (who sold GE products to customers) located in a rundown section of Caracas, Venezuela. Remembering that old credo of trying to beat the former audit cost, the hotel that was booked was probably the lowest class dive in the city. When you turned on the lights, you literally saw about one hundred cockroaches all scurrying to their homes in the baseboards. I tried to rectify this by pulling the sheets over my head, but still the next morning, I wound up with numerous cockroach bites all over my body. It got so bad that a number of us went to the senior auditor (the AIC was not there yet) and we demanded that we change hotels or we would be on the next flight back to the US.

I'm not sure if the audit staff had ever had a mutiny before. We moved that day, however, the new location would cause us to walk up and down a corridor in the city that was a known hang out for Transvestites. The advice we were given from business leaders was never walk up or down this corridor alone as it was getting close to Christmas and they needed money for buying gifts. When you get these types of warnings, you never know whether to take them seriously or "it cannot be that bad." In addition, the cockroach problem was apparently an epidemic of the entire area (including our work area because as you opened the supporting documents, out they came always scaring the shit out of you) and because moving hotels had not changed the cockroach situation.

This was historically difficult audit, It was difficult because of the (1) the language issues and (2) we did not hire translators (costs?) despite the recommendation of the last audit.

The senior auditor was a real ball buster and a problem, because all he cared about was getting in and getting back to US. He really was not concerned regarding our "in the trenches" issues, as he was only concerned about himself and his upcoming promotion. I was given accounts receivables (Barf) to review (along with some other programs). In the past, we would perform a statistical audit of the receivables balance. In this way, the computer generates a statistically valid base of accounts to verify. To verify the balance the amount owed was sent to the customer to verify that the balance was correct. Based on the outcome of the responses (the statistical result), we had always in the previous audits written, "We were unable to verify the accuracy of the accounts receivables." This result did not really help anyone other than the auditor.

The second issue was that we were relying on the postal system to send the confirmation requests and they didn't give a damn whether the mail got to the recipient or not. Looking at the previous work papers, it would be a cinch to select the statistical criteria and use the statistical percentage to calculate the amount of receivable balance and write the usual "we were unable to verify." As a result of this, I went to see the (AIC). I talked to him regarding previous results and the usual "we were unable to determine the accuracy of the accounts receivable balance because of." I indicated that the best thing for the company and shareholders would be to send out a massive amount of confirmation letters and then determine (based on returned letters) the amount of receivables we could verify.

This was a really different approach and not the usual audit recommendation. Logically, he agreed with me and gave approval to move forward using those criteria. There is an old saying that when it rains, it pours. The first problem was getting the correct balance (as the company may have had several different sub-businesses) and the correct address to mail the confirmation letters. With a tremendous amount of bad luck, the postal service went on strike. It is incredible that something so simple could become so complicated. We eventually agreed to hire private contractors to deliver the letters. This became a real cluster fuck because the private contractors could care less about how many of letters they delivered, they got paid either way so they indicated they were delivered; however, they had just simply thrown them in the trash.

We continued to conduct the audit and (as was traditional) were invited to have a cookout with the business CFO. He had a beautiful villa on the top of the hills surrounding the city. I commented on the thousands of beautiful lights that surrounded the hills. He informed me that all the lights were from the slums. Apparently, different people cut into the main electrical supply because obviously they could not afford to pay the electric bills. My thought process between the good and the bad went into overdrive as this was truly a city that hid its problems and these individuals would literally risk their lives "cutting into" the main electric line.

The audit was getting close to the scheduled end date and everyone was pulling "all nighters" to complete their programs. However, it was going to be very difficult from a pure time standpoint. Auditors were becoming angry at each other and we were also not abiding to the warnings that were given at the beginning of the audit regarding walking the corridor. Auditors were just finishing as much as they could until they just fell asleep at their desks and tried to make it back to the hotel to get some sleep. We had been there close to two and a half months and Christmas was coming up.

This audit had to be completed two weeks before Christmas for us to wrap up work papers and attend the annual Christmas Ball. We were all exhausted and not paying close attention, going to lunch one day (we only trusted one restaurant), I ordered the usual meal of fried chicken and rice. We were all talking about what we were going to do for the holidays. The meal was delivered, and it was not possible to have a chicken with that big of a leg. The waiter was smiling as I questioned that the chicken would have to be huge to produce that kind of a leg. I kept going back and forth on what I was eating was not chicken and he kept laughing and looking back at the kitchen. It caused such a big commotion that I missed looking at the rice. The rice was moving. Now this was something that could not be blame on a language barrier.

The rice was moving and the reason was that it contained live maggots. It was completely disgusting; however, I was so tired and hungry that I said screw it and started separating out the maggots so I could eat the rice.

I felt reasonably comfortable that I would not die from it. Obviously, it was just absolutely gross and I never found out where the leg came from. With the hotel and limits on how much we could spend on eating, we were reasonably assured that we would beat the cost of the previous audit. It was getting close to the end of the audit and I was just swamped with programs to conclude as I had been given others that were not going to be completed. It was about 3:00 AM, and I needed to get some sleep. I took off to the hotel (by myself), reasoning that it could not be that bad.

I started out from the business and began walking down the main corridor. I did not get too far before noticing that I had collected quite a few followers. The option to turn back was gone. I could not go back without confronting this group of transvestites behind me. The only option was to go forward. The hotel always seemed a shorter distance in the morning, but tonight, it was feeling extremely long. As I moved forward, I realized that I had been flanked on either side and again the only option was forward. I was getting closer and closer. As I rounded the turn to the hotel, I was hoping that they would fall back out of sight.

I could not have been more wrong. They knew that I did not have many options because when I got to the front door, it had been chained shut with no one around to open the door. The group of individuals began to salivate and my situation became more critical. The more I banged and shouted to get in, they were getting braver moving up the front steps to grab me. At this time around Christmas, they were out to jump any tourist take their valuables and then stab them to ensure they didn't get immediate help. I was now panicking when I heard a voice coming from the bushes below saying, "Señor, Señor." It was the "bell hop" that was usually in the lobby. He told me to come with him to safety. This decision was not hard because the alternative was no option at all.

I jump down into the bushes that covered the front of the hotel and ran with him into the parking garage. We went into an elevator that went up to the top of the garage (around eight stories) by now he explained to me that they had to keep the door chained closed that late at night and we were almost to safety inside the hotel. There was only one problem left. The buildings were not connected (shit). He kept saying no problem sir it is easy, you just had to walk about eight to ten feet from building to building on what looked like a two by eight (but in reality was probably a four by eight). He went first to show me that it was not difficult just do not look down. I was already panicked so it was just go for it (I think I had already shit my pants). When I reached the other side, I was on the roof of the hotel and it was a simple task of going to my room.

Tonight the cockroaches did not seem that bad. I told myself never again, I lied down and fell asleep from sheer exhaustion. The next day I made sure the rest of the team would not make that same mistake. It was getting closer and closer to Christmas and our departure. The decision to try to verify as much of the receivable balance as we could was now looking like a poor decision, as we just didn't consider that people and companies did not give a shit to validate the amounts and if they did, the postal service or private delivery companies could care less whether this "mailing" was important. We wrote up all the defects in the processes and balances.

The main asset of receivables was still an issue. That last night, as it turned to dawn, we went to one of the larger buildings in the area to see the sunrise. From that height, it looked truly beautiful and all the shitty issues seemed to melt away. However, I made the mistake of looking down and there was a group of individuals bathing completely naked in the fountain, this truly was "God's hell hole" on earth (or one of them). As we wrapped it up and headed for the airport, we encountered our usual departure through immigration of "Señor, your passport is not in order," getting it back and slipping in the usual twenty dollars was greeted with "Señor, your passport is now in order." Quickly through the terminal and into our seats, most of us bought a drink and slept the remainder of the flight.

The time while you were at the "office" was a zoo as the entire staff was on a single floor. You just grabbed any seat that you could find. You spent the remaining time wrapping up and writing appraisals and loose audit papers before getting your next audit assignment. We split doing cleanup of files and wrapping programs and signing off on its completion. The time for the audit leaders was spent supervising the wrap up and writing the appraisals. Most of the audit teams were back by the tenth of December and completed the wraps until around December 22 when we went on break and didn't fly out to our next assignments until after January 3 or 4. During this time, two critical things were completed. First, you were given your appraisal and had a discussion of potential and the second was your next audit assignment.

Prior to this audit, I had always received outstanding appraisals. This was important because anyone with any brains would look at the individual's history to check for consistency. On this audit, The AIC and the senior auditor were going to lay the receivable blow up squarely on me. I was given a poor review, which basically would end my career on staff just at the end of my second year. The assumption by all managers was that the cream would always rise to the top. At this time, you were either going to be promoted to a senior auditor or not. The importance of this event would determine how far you would go in your career. Looking for a job as a semi-senior meant that you did not get the career boost that generally we all hoped for. As background, you had the first year as a junior auditor; second year as a semi-senior, third year as a senior auditor and last as a supervisor or AIC.

The world of Finance in GE looked at when you came off staff when interviewing for any job. It would follow your career forever. The first question was always why did you only reach semi-senior auditor? The answer to that question determined your long-term career aspects. The good thing was that all appraisals were reviewed by the Audit Administrators. I was called into one of four audit administrator's office and was given a copy of my appraisal. It was highly inflammatory and was the result of the decision to validate the receivable balance. Just about every section of the appraisal was a poor performance. I was going to take the fall on the decision of the verification of receivables.

I was requested to comment on the appraisal. I disagreed with the appraisal as it was based on not just me making the decision on receivables when in fact it was a team decision. It was also in conflict with my previous seven appraisals in which I had been given an outstanding rating. All hell broke loose. He brought in the AIC and the senior auditor and asked for an explanation of the appraisal. When they started to justify their appraisal with the receivable decision, he reminded them that the methodology used was approved by all above and not just me. They were told to rewrite the appraisal for his approval. Many of the negative comments were removed and the decision regarding receivables was a team decision.

I believe that the appraisal ended up as an excellent appraisal, one step down from outstanding. It was also decided that there was enough remaining work left in the audit that the senior, myself, and another semi-senior auditor were going to be extended for another three months. When I was told that I would be extended (going back for at least a month and maybe three) for completion of the Venezuela audit, I was not happy. The fact that I would be working with the same senior auditor, put a real damper on the annual Christmas ball and remaining holidays.

We took off for Caracas again and were booked into the same hotel, and the roaches were still there as well as in the documents given to you by the client. My job was to complete as much of the receivable balance review that I could. After another three weeks, we were able to extrapolate what the statistical number of errors that we could expect. Although we were unable to statistically validate the balance, we were able to physically verify a large balance of the receivables.

After getting agreement from the client's management, the three of us rapidly completed the remaining audit programs, we were able to complete the audit. We spent the last evening, sitting on the roof in lawn chairs and drank beer while watching the sunset. We had the audit documents sent to Schenectady for peer review and filing. We spent the usual games getting our passports in order before getting on the plane for the return. As we were rolling down the runway, I gave the entire city the finger without being seen. It was still a hellhole!

I join my last audit in about a month and a half (coming from Caracas) into a three month review of Housewares' so I wasn't exactly going to get the best audit programs but instead given all those small two-day reviews that were needed for completion. I had been on the corporate audit staff for a little over two years when my spouse decided to drop a "bombshell' and said that she had enough and gave me the ultimate demand to request off the audit staff or separate with her taking the baby. This was ironic because of the amount of audits that were in town or close.

She had only experienced thirteen and a half months of out of town audits. She really hadn't had the hardship of the normal audit staff wife. This usually does not come as a surprise to the auditor or audit staff when there were issues with the appraisals indicating that further advancement would not take place, however in cases that the audit staff had more plans for you in the future, it becomes more difficult to request off (especially when it is a surprise). I had mixed feelings because I knew what I was giving up and what requesting off would do to my career path. I was requested to come to headquarters to "talk to a couple of audit administrators." The first told me that they would be sorry for me not to continue on Staff. He also indicated that if it was about becoming a senior auditor that they could make that happen today as they had been happy with my progress and felt reasonably comfortable about my future career path.

The second Audit Administrator was more upset and abrupt (less professional) and felt like I was springing a surprise on the staff. We continued to discuss that it was about my marriage and small child and the impact to me personally if I chose to stay on and my spouse left. He then made a bad decision when he asked me "if I was always going to let my wife make my career decisions." That pretty well cleared up any bad feelings that I had about leaving. We completed the day with the realization that I was going to request off and would become a candidate competing with those who were informed that their time with the audit staff had concluded. As jobs came up, a slate of auditors coming off was provided to the hiring manager. I also informed my spouse that if she ever asked me to do something that would limit my career advancement again that we would be done and go our separate ways.

To be blunt, you have spent your last five years (including FMP) busting your ass days, nights, and week-ends to be promoted as far as you could and as fast as you could. My "fast track" career was over, and I would now have to do it the hard way to get to the same position as I would have provided that I would have traveled for four years. The gauntlet had fallen early on my advancement, thanks to my wife. I would now get to take the traditional route of getting a new promotion every two years and filling in the blanks you needed to round out your abilities. The normal process was to spend around two years on each "level" and climb the ladder two years at a time. The Company had a rather archaic level system which went from seven to twenty-three.

At any time that you were not promoted in two years, you knew your future career prospects were limited. The audit staff let you skip this two year process and basically, if you came off after two years it would be as a level 10 to 11 versus a level 8 or 9 without having travelled on the staff. That was not a bad trade off, but you would forever be explaining to future hiring managers why you did not go further than two years on the audit staff. (It was guaranteed as the first question of the interview.) If you went further and were able to become an AIC, you would be coming off staff at an executive level (15 or above).

It was clearly a risk /reward that gave you the benefit of all that sacrifice. A level 15 (the company later gave up this archaic level system that everyone measured their career against). They develop a system where levels 7–14 were professional band, 15–17 were executive positions, and 18–21 were considered senior executive band, after that you became a vice president. This new system allowed you to take jobs that were important for your career without measuring which exact level it was. It was important from a pay and bonuses package as the package for level

15 and above was eligible for your base pay plus bonus and possibly stock options, also in the executive band and above, you were also eligible for the first of three executive business leadership courses. GE Capital had its own system and a VP in Capital was not the same as a VP in the company they also had their own audit staff.

The reason I go through this level system now is to show how much getting to the top was on the audit staff. The further you stayed on and got promoted was correlated with the level of job slates that you would be interviewing for. It was critical that you get further ahead on the audit staff so that you would come off at a higher level and basically jump the levels because of your audit staff experience. If you only went for two years at your decision or the audit staff's decision then all that sacrifice and all those overnighters didn't pay off as much. Again, the system was always assuming that the cream rose to the top.

While I waited to be notified of any job interviews, I continued to help out the teams various audit programs. At that time, I was given a job interview for running GE Televisions internal audit staff. I met the CFO and his leadership team who I really felt good about becoming part of his team. I was offered the position (I believe at a level 11) and accepted. Two weeks later, the audit team had taken me to my "farewell" dinner and we had quite a few drinks. I spent the following days cleaning up, saying goodbyes and thanking all those that had helped my career. I was also arranging getting everything ready to move from Schenectady to Portsmouth, Virginia. My career on audit staff was over and now I would have to work even harder to get the same position as I would have if I had stayed longer.

I have spent much time discussing the audit staff as it was such a huge professional opportunity. It was known as a fast-track program for financial executives and every outside recruiter new it. It was because on every audit, you were thrown into the deep end to see if you could swim. I always was amazed that on every audit I was able to come up with a plan to accomplish the audit. You were also able to view individual's leadership styles, and last, you had the ability to network on every audit. The reason that the audit staff worked was because of the above. No one got promoted based on their ability to wrap audit programs. But because of the assignments and how well you worked, you were also on your way to developing your own leadership style. One of the key attributes that you were measured against was being a congenial member of the group, not only with your peers, but by the business leaders you met.

The reason that individuals fight so hard to get on the audit staff was that when you stepped back from it, it was the only place in the world that would allow you to see many businesses, their strategies, their leadership and what was working and what was not. Overall, you got (1) promoted rapidly, (2) met the business leaders of the businesses that you audited (networking), and (3) understood which business's had a viable business plan and those that didn't. Also, the development process did not matter which business function you came from. You had the luxury to think about the businesses you were auditing, looking at the finance organizations of successful leaders. Talking to these various finance positions, you can recognize who had the talent working for them and how successful his or hers leadership style was on the organization not only as a CFO but as a valued part of business staff.

It happened right around the middle of when I was on audit staff. Jack Welch was named CEO replacing Reginald Jones. At the time of his appointment, he reported to a group and eventually to GE's CEO. Jack knew that he was in consideration to replace Reg; he was a brilliant business leader that demanded results. This was such an important announcement that they had brought in every auditor from the field to see the announcement together. It was a shock, everyone had liked and became accustomed to the way Reg developed and grown the company (comfortable with the status quo). Jack was the complete opposite of Reg Jones. Reg wanted someone different that would take the company in a new direction. Jack understood how, at every layer of management the more distanced you were from understanding the real issues that faced the business because at every level the issues became more sugar coated. Now consider the sheer numbers of "executives" and strategic planners that it took to develop a business pitch to Jack. He quickly disbanded all of these layers so that for any business, the business leader would not be more than one or two levels from reporting to him. He needed business leaders that were faster and more nimble to react to markets that were changing at a more rapid pace in order to survive the developing and changing global markets.

Out went all of those useless reporting levels that took forever to move. This saved the company hundreds of millions on all the individuals' compensation and business reports. These constant reports really did not benefit a business as the closer it got to Jack, the more benign it became. It also improved profitability for being able to execute faster. Next came the "become number 1 or 2 in your industry" or be prepared to fix or sell the business. Again, there came an incredible amount of reports about where you stood in your "market." Because these two changes by themselves allowed him to take out so many people, he gained the title of "Neutron Jack," which deep down, he hated. Most employees never looked at a bigger picture as by delayering the businesses and leadership he was creating a much more competitive Company. This gave more job protection to the remaining employees. Listening to his announcement, it was critical for the audit staff to change and become more focused on critical issues and processes.

CHAPTER 6

Video Products

The move to Portsmouth, Virginia, was slightly different in that all your costs (within reason) for moving were covered by the company, however, the interest rates to buy homes wasn't. The nation was into a period of hyperinflation with interest rates on homes at 15–25 percent. You were doing many different financing schemes to buy a house at the lowest interest rate you could find (15–18 percent interest). We got lucky in finding a house that we could do a wrap-around "bundled" interest, which kept the lower interest rate of the previous owner with the current rate of 15–16 percent. As we got to the day before closing, the closing fell apart because the individual had misrepresented his loan, and it could not be wrapped. Fortunately, the house two doors down was a loan, which could be wrapped and the veterinarian was willing to work with us on a fairly short notice.

We were able to close on our first house and move in. I spent the next two years doing basic audit program work on parts of the business and constantly doing warehouse inventory audits. I was also able to meet the key financial leaders. I spent a lot of time with the manager of accounting operations and the manager of cost accounting. Both were long-term employees of the business who were always available as a sounding board. The definition of the internal audit staff was myself and one FMP. We knew that inventory was being stolen, but how? I even spent some nights doing surveillance including behind the warehouse, which was backed up against the Chesapeake Bay. The business also had businesses in Singapore and Malaysia (both of which I audited). I traveled to both of these businesses.

I spent about three days in Singapore and the first night I went to eat at a place the concierge recommended. I ordered an appetizer of mushrooms. The first one I ate didn't taste good but I brushed it off as being in a foreign country. I woke up in the middle of the night puking my guts out. It just wouldn't stop, and by morning, it was coming out of both ends. I had never encountered food poisoning. It took three days to where I could walk again. I finished up my work in Singapore and I went north with another finance person in the business through Malaysia. The business was excited because I was one of the few corporate executives from their perspective to come to the business.

I spent the morning listening to business reports and the afternoon on a plant tour. In between was lunch where I had requested to eat with the factory personnel. They had laid out some traditional dishes of which I asked for the least spicy hot. They gave me a dish and the first bite brought tears to my eyes. It was so hot. I was determined not to give in and finished the dish. It was a nice review, and we traveled back to Singapore where I got a plane back to the US. It was a nice trip except for the food poisoning.

In all the audits that I performed, I never did catch any thieves, but I did get to see the way that the company treated CFOs in the business that didn't agree with their CEO. I say this from a low-level perspective. The first thing that I was able to learn was that the CFO's style should conform to the CEO's style. In our case, he had sent a new business leader that had the attitude that you were either with him or against him. Jack had hired him based on his pure intellect. He needed someone who could understand where the television and video product markets were going as they were changing at an accelerated pace with increasing foreign competition. He had a number of business "parties" to understand who he wanted on his team. Unfortunately, the CFO did not agree with the new CEO's "vision" or style and was not in his camp.

So it came down to an either he goes or I do and he had their first business meeting with "Fairfield." The next morning, we were told by our CFO that a new CFO had been named for the business and that he had taken early retirement. This had to of been in the works for a while. I went through this over and over in my mind and concluded that if you had a disagreement with the CEO, you had better work it out before you got in front of Jack. I was also very conflicted because I felt a progressive company should value the inputs of individuals that didn't necessarily agree. Anyway, he told me that he would be more than okay and to not be concerned about his future. I did know that he had a girlfriend within the business. I can still be extremely thankful for his insights about the market and business. He was professional to the last day.

Shortly thereafter, I was asked to go to headquarters to evaluate my further potential. I was more worried about how to find this "bunker" location than what was going to happen. It had been a very late arrival because of weather. I got to the hotel around 2:00 a.m. with an arrival at headquarters at 7:30 a.m. I arrived to have multiple interviews by corporate HR personnel. The discussion was what business/financial strengths would be best to develop my career. We had a large discussion concerning my needing to fine tune my perceived strengths and weaknesses to improve my future resume to become a CFO by taking a manager of cost accounting position. They went through all the benefits of taking a job they had to fill. I went through all the ways cost accounting could cause me numerous problems. Their final salvo was that I would never be a successful CFO without punching this ticket.

Flying home that night, I listed all the reasons of why I did not want to take the job. It came down to that I was scared that my performance would not be the best thing for my career given my previous experiences with this field. I also knew their decision was that I had to take the position to demonstrate my abilities in this field. I had to beat my "demons." We both came down to the same conclusion. Take the job.

CHAPTER 7

Coshocton, Ohio

I became manager of the cost accounting group for the Laminated Business reporting to a CFO that would not take "no" for an answer. Ed also knew that if you had done your best and communicated frequently, you would do fine. He just came across as stern; and demanded that you should always try to figure out how to fix the problem. I had a great staff who quickly knew that they had "a lot" to teach me and it was a lot of fun learning cost accounting with a group of experts. We discussed what cost accounting was supposed to be, and what inventory values were considering LIFO and FIFO versus standards and actuals and how it would all come together. Around this time, I realized that you could not properly do a good job unless you became a significant partner with the manufacturing leadership.

Prior to this, cost accounting was just a bunch of "number crunchers." I change the name of the organization to manufacturing finance with the responsibility of supporting both finance and manufacturing. We became a partner with manufacturing being able to support all the books and records, but also sitting in on the manufacturing teams weekly staff meetings. A significant event changed a paradigm that finance was not out to always make manufacturing the scapegoat. If manufacturing had a problem then the business had a problem. All of us then became a team to solve the issue with the lowest cost impact. It took the manufacturing leader as well as the finance manager to be broad enough to see the benefits of this type of change.

During this time, we also hired two financial management program (FMPs) to the organization. The female FMPs happened to be "knockouts" in a very, very small city. Everyone knew everyone else's business. There was absolutely no privacy. One of the first things I had to do, being in charge of the FMP program, was to find them adequate doctor care in a neighboring city to prevent everyone from knowing everything about them. Both of them were excellent FMPs not only in the assignments but also in class which they traveled to Columbus to take.

We had made really close friends with some neighbors down the street (not with GE). Ron and I played golf a lot and neither of us was very good but we had fun cheating on our scores. We spent a lot of time eating at one another's houses. On Saturday nights, we usually played cards and drank until around midnight. He was always helpful when I was screwing up fixes to the house and property and we continued our friendship all through my stay at Coshocton. Later on when I was on special assignment in Columbus, I learned that Ron had come home from work and sat down to dinner when he suddenly fell forward and died of a massive coronary. Life really is short. He left his wife and three small boys.

It wasn't easy making friends in such a small community and you relied heavily on your managers at work to break up the time. I played a lot of golf with both the finance and manufacturing managers. We played separately because they were always at odds with each other. This was the first time that I had to balance two extremely different people who didn't really like each other.

Turning to the financial side, we had the responsibility to hedge copper prices (the single largest cost in the business.) Unfortunately, we hedged copper to rise and it went down. It continued down and at the end of the year, we wound out to be triple hedged in copper. In GE, we were not supposed to use hedging as a profit maker. We were supposed (through the use of hedges) to establish a hedge that would validate the operating plan in both quantity and price. We kept doubling down as prices continued to slide down. Needless to say, we got a "significant reprimand" and started with new routines the next year.

That next year, we got a new business leader who was very good and respected the finance organization. I was promoted to the leader of financial planning and analysis (FP&A) of the Laminated Business, another stepping stone to further promotion. Our finance manager (CFO) was promoted to a group CFO. My new responsibilities would include doing the short-term and long-term business plans and reporting short-term business results, which were shared with the business and sent to group for consolidation. I like working with the new CFO and CEO on the business plans but it was to be short-lived.

I had completed many home projects at our residence in Coshocton. Some were easy and some not so easy. In order to clean up the property of dead wood, I bought a chainsaw. I was doing pretty good one Saturday and got more careless as I went along. So I was cutting up small branches and rather holding the saw with both hands, I was just using my left hand and the chainsaw kicked back and my right hand immediately went to block my face. The chainsaw caught me in my hand between my little finger and palm. We quickly made a trip to the emergency room where the only thing they could do was bandage it up. A chainsaw does not make a cut. It just chews up the flesh.

My next project was to be able to mow the lawn and the field behind the house to the woods. I went to the Sears store and bought a riding lawn mower. Well, the neighbors started a pool as to how long it would take me to overturn the tractor. When I got home, I got the tractor ready. One of the things on my list was to remove a large hedge in the front yard. So I forgot all about the laws of physics and tied the rope to the back of the tractor and to the hedge. I put it in drive and because the hedge wouldn't move but the tires would I went straight up and over. Thanks goodness the tractor had a dead man's switch. Whoever had less than an hour won the pool. Of course, the proper way was to attach the rope to the front and pull backward so the tires would dig in and pull it out.

The next project was painting the house. It was going pretty well and again the more that I did the more careless

LESSONS OF EXPERIENCE

I became. I kept moving the ladder in the front from left to right, I came to the bay window and because it wasn't flat I had to extend the ladder higher to clear the window. I got started and it wasn't long for the bottom of the ladder to start sliding as the angle was just too much. The ladder slipped down and I went through the Bay windows and into the house along with all the paint.

Once again, it was something that you do all the time which is change the tire. I got everything ready and jacked up the car and took the tire off. Well, the asphalt driveway couldn't handle the weight and the car came down on my leg.

Finally, when I was actually in Columbus, I needed to put on a chimney cap. So I went to the hardware store and bought one that from the instructions looked simple. So I got home and went out on the roof through the bathroom window. The cap was square and the instructions were to push on both sides until it fit the chimney. Well, it didn't account for the hot day and sweat on my hands. I applied the force with my hands to make the cap smaller and my hand slipped. It cut all the way down to the bone; well my hand was spurting out blood with every pulse. I wrapped my other hand around it trying to slow the blood and kept calling for my wife. Also, I could not get back into the bathroom window without letting go of my hand. I got through the window, but now the bathroom was covered in blood.

Thank goodness that my next door neighbor was a medic in the army. He was able to slow the bleeding so that we could get to the hospital. The doctor walked in and began examining the cut and how deep it went. She then took the finger and pulled back to see how deep it was. I felt terrible pain and flesh tearing. They were able to stich it all up but wanted to wait for two days to see if I cut any nerves. I went to a specialist who determined that I had cut some nerves and would require surgery to re attach them.

Two days later, I had to go into surgery to reattach them. I went to the hospital that day with a terrible migraine headache. As we were preparing for a nerve block instead of anesthesia, I mentioned to the doctor that it would be wonderful to get rid of the headache. He said don't worry and the next thing I knew was it was gone. The rest of the surgery went fine and I walked out with a major bandaged hand.

Well, with each of these incidents, somehow I had to travel to make presentations to Jack and I was always in some kind of bandages. After the chimney cap incidence, he looked across at me with those steely blue eyes and asked me if he paid me enough money. I responded yes (what else was I going to say) and he said hire contractors to do the house projects as he was tired of seeing me in bandages. I was glad that he cared about my health.

CHAPTER 8

Diamonds

Shortly after being named to the FP&A position in Coshocton, I was requested by the Group Finance leader (my previous CFO at Laminated) with the concurrence of Dennis Dammerman to complete a short-term assignment, which was simple, go in and determine if the Diamond Business (part of my last CFO's group) was calculating transfer prices correctly between the Manufacturing operations (located in Columbus, Ohio, and Dublin, Ireland) and that there was consistency between the two manufacturing plants to blend product offerings.

I went in and perform a very cursory overview, interviewing cost personnel, financial analysts, engineers, finance manager, and the CEO. My conclusion and recommendations were that there could be an issue and that a much-deeper review was needed which included the corporate audit staff (to yield independence) and the tax organization (expertise). It was determined that this team would be run by me. This quickly became a personal battle between the group financial manager and the president of the business.

(They hated each other and would do anything to ruin the other person's career.)

I was required to give many interim reports to the group leadership. They were at "odds" with the business leader because he wanted to run the business without group's input. Emotions all around were strained; we had to give frequent updates at all hours of the night and day. It was not uncommon to be sitting on the back porch of the group's CFO giving the latest update. These updates (when they supported the group's position) were immediately shared with the top leadership in GE. Otherwise, we just got a good dinner.

There were several issues here, the first being a dislike of a business CEO that would not share critical information regarding the business. The second issue was to determine the correct way to value transfer pricing of diamonds from the US to Ireland and from Ireland to the US. As this valuation was critical because Ireland was a tax-free country and any income derived in Ireland was not taxed. The net income was consolidated back to the business at 100 percent. This business was creating a lot of income to the group and ultimately the corporation, I was about to be caught in a real donnybrook between business leaders that had no love loss for each other in addition to ensuring that we had no issues with our transfer pricing.

In conducting this review, we had read numerous interpretations of the correct way to determine transfer pricing according to the IRS and proper accounting. This required a significant review in documentation of how to develop transfer pricing and proper application across all the business components. Several methodologies could have been interpreted as correct.

It became clear that the business management had a pretty good idea that the methodology they were using was solely to generate as much income as possible, regardless of the current methodology recommended by the IRS. As a result, it was necessary to review who knew what and where. The CFO had left General Electric, so we were left with the manager of accounting and the manager of cost accounting to determine how the current way of determining valuation was derived and the associated impact that it had on the business and group net income. It was complicated because you valued each size (crystal) from a machine batch. These different sizes and strengths were blended to provide product to our customers. We provided these diamonds to manufactures that produced saw blades, drill bits, and other applications. These were manmade diamonds that were used in coatings.

The personalities of the parties involved were very different. The Diamond's CEO was stoic, polite, and professional. The best analogy was that he was a perfect English gentleman. On the contrary, the manager of accounting was the complete opposite. He was aloof, not forthcoming, and deliberately led you down incorrect paths. In short, he was a real asshole. As we conducted each interview, we were establishing a timeline to determine who knew what and when. The manager of cost accounting was very knowledgeable of the processes that the business was currently using. You could tell that he did not want to disclose any knowledge of wrongdoing.

The manager of accounting was guiding him. It was also necessary to spend a significant amount of time with the chief engineer who not only invented the processes to separate batches but was the same man that invented how to make man made diamonds. I spent much time learning the how of taking carbon and placing it into carbide die's (these were huge to replicate the process of intense heat and pressure to turn the carbon into diamonds). Not every batch was a success if the carbide die's blew. The engineers would go to work to see what happened. The pressure that was built up into these dies was incredible. Therefore, every analysis was different. I found this engineer to be extremely smart but had a hard time explaining things in simple terms.

The chief accountant and I started out with very polite and cordial conversations, the further that we went on, our discussions became much more difficult. The more I talked with him the more suspicious I became of anything he told me. I knew that if I gave him enough rope that he would eventually hang himself; you could only describe his conduct as being arrogant and incorrect. Every time we met, he immediately went to the CEO's office to do a debrief. We knew something was not being properly explained. We spent many days and nights going through multiple pricing transactions to determine consistency and potential errors. It also required a trip to the Dublin, Ireland (which we did not mind at all and came back loaded with Lennox, China), to discuss the ramifications of the current processes in the business, and what the leadership in this subsidiary knew and when.

The business leadership in Ireland was very helpful and forthcoming. It was there that the CFO of the business taught me the difference between a scheme and a sham. The first was just stretching accounting rules, which would be likely approved by the independent auditors and determined correct. A sham was just plain wrong. He was a delightful person whose knowledge I respected (we would continue our respect for each other for many years). On one trip, he took me to play golf at the Royal Dublin golf course. It was the first time I had played on a Links course and I was terrible. You just could not imagine in your dreams how deep the bunkers were and how challenging the course could be.

I played terrible and eventually stopped keeping score and just enjoyed the few good shots that I had. It was a delightful day and further solidified my appreciation of the CFO. We took the knowledge that we learned in Ireland and went back to the business. But not before we rented a car and went as far north into Northern Ireland as we could. We made it a day trip and it was just exquisite countryside as green as emeralds. I had to admit my fear of terrorists crept into my mind but as we got closer to Belfast, my fears were not warranted.

There was an incredible amount of data to sort through and apply to the business at the same time the manager of accounting became less and less forthcoming. During all of this, it required numerous communications between the companies leadership. It was not just a simple open and shut case. Because the evaluation and separation of a batch of diamonds coming down the separating machine in which diamonds fell into different grades (that would never be sold on their own).

The various sizes and grades would be mixed to determine a product that could be sold. How much and in what quantity this mixture occurred would determine the products and eventual profitability of what the business sold and as I noted before, it was also necessary to spend a considerate amount of time with the engineer who designed the process of how to create manmade diamonds and how they were separated to create useful batches that could be made into product. Every time you thought you got something, you would have to go back and verify its accuracy as every step was interrelated.

These diamonds were made to the use in mixtures (grades and sizes) for cutting or grinding applications such as saw blades and other cutting products (for instance the blades to cut up concrete highways). We just continued to go back and forth with the questioning; however, something did not make sense and we were determined to find out what it was. We began by looking at the entries used to close the books every month. It still did not make much sense and he was not going to be helpful.

I knew I was hitting a nerve because the meetings between he and the CEO and his staff became more frequent and his distaste for me even more profound. I continued looking at journal entries focusing on the closing entries. Something was wrong. There were always closing entries that modified the accounts so that they would hit exactly what they committed to the group on net income (which was always lower than what the group needed to hit their commitment to corporate). Was it possible that they were keeping two sets of books? I kept pushing and he finally had just enough.

He confirmed that there were two sets of books. With this knowledge, group management were peeing in their pants (they were so excited that they would finally get this guy). It just made my life extremely more complex. I then had to determine who knew what within finance. It was clear that the manager of accounting operations would be terminated immediately and I had no qualms of performing that termination. It was the manager of cost accounting that I was concerned about. This situation was held so close to the vest that I was worried that if we terminated him, we would lose any trail to correct all the entries. We reached an agreement that if he helped us with all the correcting entries and other impacts that we would keep him on.

We then spent about a month (1) correcting the accounts and records; (2) developing a proper transfer price procedure (approved by the IRS); (3) developing a presentation to the government which would lay out what happened, the impact on net income, and taxes and the action taken regarding individuals which were involved; and (4) how we would establish a new leadership team and accounting processes to fix the issues going forward.

I had set up an appointment to see the CEO. We had a professional conversation where he indicated that he knew about the issues. I asked him what he would do next and he indicated maybe consulting work within the industry as he was very well respected and liked. We both knew that this would be his last day in the office, as he would be immediately locked out. He asked me if he could give me some advice. I said yes, as I honestly was interested in what he was going to say. He indicated that he was very impressed with my technical and financial skills and the review that I had done in a very tough environment.

He thanked me for keeping my professionalism and not engaging in the mudslinging. He then said that I was much too smart and had a very promising career to use foul language (four-letter words) to make my point. He indicated how unprofessional it sounded and I should resist using that vocabulary. I thanked him for his feedback (as upon reflecting on it, he was correct). I wished him well. He would now start his negotiations on his separation agreement with the corporation. Upon conclusion, the auditor and tax individuals went back to their previous positions. There is also a saying that no good deed goes unpunished. It was concluded (by group and Dennis Dammerman) that who better to fix everything than the person that dug it all up. I was then promoted as the new manager of accounting operations and financial planning and analysis (this was temporary until I could interview with the proper management to be appointed as the new manager of finance for Diamond Business.

I moved the family to Columbus, Ohio, and found a beautiful house just northeast of the city. As the new manager of finance, I was responsible for all the financials to be consolidated into the Plastics Group. I also had the responsibility for the short and long range plans for the business. I developed an excellent team of financial individuals for the business as well as preparing all of the short-term budgets and long-range forecasts. I was also responsible for implementing the tax recommendations that we had made. It was a fun job, and I worked for a new CEO of the business Ed Russell.

We got along well and had no major conflicts. The name of the business became GE Superabrasives instead of Diamonds. Both Dennis and Jack were laughing at the similarities of the new name of the business and the personalities of two individuals in the company. They were joking whether if the business was more appropriately named after me or another leader in GE. It had to be one or the other. The humor did not go unnoticed by many people, as neither of us was known for having "great personalities." We executed on our commitments to Corporate but were somewhat abrasive in doing so. I reflected on this and decided that I needed to become less abrasive if I wanted to succeed.

Unfortunately, toward the end of this assignment, there was an incident with our neighbors. We were going on vacation, and we asked the next door neighbors son to watch the house. We had left a key so that if he had to go into the house it was available. When we returned, my wife noticed that someone had gone through her underwear drawer. She confronted the teenager that we asked to watch the house and he admitted to doing it. The parents determined a punishment for the teenager. My wife didn't believe that it was enough for what he did but rather than work it out with the neighbors, she called the police. I had asked her not to do it but she insisted that she was right.

They arrested the teenager and his mother went apoplectic. She ranted and raved at my wife for what she had done.

Over the next several months, this woman would sit on our property line in a chair and every time we came out of the house and she would just glare at us. It became unbearable and I dreaded coming home or leaving for work not to mention the entire weekend. Of course it did not go unnoticed by all the other neighbors. She made it her point in life to make us miserable. I built a fence in our backyard so I wouldn't have to see her but she only moved to the front yard.

So eventually we had to go to go to family court where the teenager was sentence by the judge. Of course whatever sentence he got would be sealed by the court and would not carry with him forever. At this point rather than her just accepting what had been done, she just continued to make our lives miserable. I had asked my wife not to do it and was mad at her for creating such a miserable environment. Fortunately at this point I was interviewing for a new position, which I got so I was able to move away from the confrontation. I learned to just leave your neighbors alone.

CHAPTER 9

GE Programs Finance

This position required technical skills of FP&A, cost accounting, and managing five program finance individuals (mini CFOs). I would report to the CFO, Dan with the requirements of interfacing with each of the business units. It was a somewhat complex matrix organization where the business units would be responsible for their business plans and utilize the rest of the business for support.

I stayed on top of the manufacturing finance personnel and the support that they gave to the business. My biggest concern was that the manager of cost accounting would retire and the institutional knowledge that he had would leave with him. Fortunately, he decided to stay which allowed me to pursue my real interest in developing a matrix organization called the programs finance organization that consisted of four separate businesses (small motors, large motors, commercial and heating and air-conditioning organization in the business along with two Korean JVs).

The Koreans respected their military leadership and many businesses had an ex-military CEOs. I was the programs finance manager and sat on both businesses board of directors. It was a dichotomy with the US moving to a matrix organization and the organization structure of the joint ventures. I attended the quarterly board meetings. Determining when we would see continual profits and decreased cash requirements. The issues always required capital to make the business operate. Unfortunately, we couldn't always trust the Koreans with our current production and technology so they always had the previous version of technology. As we were concerned that the patents and manufacturing expertise would transfer to their control. They thought nothing toward reverse engineering. We wanted a partner not a competitor. Unfortunately, neither JV was coming up to speed as quickly as a GE expected.

There were other issues concerning the joint ventures, their leadership in the joint ventures was senior ex-military (late fifties or early sixties) whereas, I was in my early thirties. This created issues because of my age differential. Our president and CEO David informed them that I was the selection to sit on the board of directors and there was no discussion on this point. The other issue was when they had an objection or disagreement in the board meetings was to just get up and walk out of the meetings. This would be a stall tactic and one that was used and the only way to control this behavior was that when I had objections, I would get up and walk out. When this happened, they quickly realized that I was not fooling around.

These two military leaders (one for each venture) managed by fear. They were brutal with their employees and their behavior was questionable. During one board meeting, the secretary messed up on the delivery of beverages.

The next day, I noticed that this secretary had a black eye. I asked her what had happened and she indicated that the CEO had hit her. For a business leader to do this (hit a secretary) was unacceptable behavior. In the board meeting, I made it clear that this was unacceptable behavior, which would not be tolerated. After the board meeting, I called back to the business leaders and advised them of what happened and along with this and other leadership issues with the startup, we requested a change in leadership of the joint venture. He was gone and a lot of employees were happy.

One of the favorable tactics for the southern joint venture was to take the GE personnel out for drinks and dinner. The goal was to take shots of Sojo (an alcoholic drink) and for each person to take a bite of a jalapeño pepper. This game was to see how long the GE employees would last. But the peppers were just too hot for me but I didn't want to not participate. I asked them why they were so hot to GE personnel and not to the Koreans. It all came down to how you bit into the peppers; we would take a bite at the end of the pepper cutting across all the veins.

They would take a bite from the side, horizontally, and cut through less veins and therefore making it significantly milder. Dinner was the usual and always with too much garlic. Trust me one of the things you didn't want to do was wake up in the middle of the night, hung over, and sweating out garlic. Even when you got on the airplane to come home the smell of garlic was incredible. One of their favorite meals was kimchi, which was made by taking cabbage and other ingredients and burying it in the backyard until it fermented. It didn't taste that bad but the smell was terrible. To this day, I can always detect the smell of this "staple diet."

It took a long time for these joint ventures to come up to speed. Another "duty" of this job was to buy fake Rolex watches. They certainly looked real but had quartz movements. Everyone always wanted one. So I usually picked an afternoon and went shopping loading up on watches. I was giving one of the watches to one of my employees when the CEO walked in. He asked who would want a fake Rolex (he was wearing his real Rolex presidential). My employee responded who would be stupid enough to pay for a real Rolex. His career became limited as long as David was running the business.

One of the mentors that I had in motors was the vice president of sales, Roger. I had been the programs finance manager for two years. He came up to me and said it was about time that I have a real job. He talked to me about becoming the leader of the heating and air-conditioning sales operation (HVAC). This was an organization that had $345 million in sales, and I would be responsible for both the sales organization and marketing. I had never thought about leaving finance but the opportunity to become more experienced was too great to pass up. GE was working to broaden me and give me a new experience (also to broaden my personality).

The two years that I was responsible for HVAC was unfortunate because of a severely depressed sales market (housing), which was either down or flat. My customers were Carrier, Trane, York, Rheem, Lennox, and Bristol. I tried to focus on the variables to be successful. The first was competitive pricing and the second was just in time inventory. Unfortunately, we were just not there from a reliable product flow without stockpiling. We would put inventory close to their manufacturing sites; however, one of the worst things that could and did happen a couple of times was for customers to run out of inventory requiring them to shut down their lines and send employees home. When this happened, you had some pretty intense conversations and reactions to get inventory there ASAP. After the dust settled, it usually required dinners with both me and Roger giving assurances that it wouldn't happen again. They usually wanted to take the opportunity to spend the time negotiating price and share. Roger was masterful in handling complex issues with customers and I learned a lot from him.

Roger was a fantastic sales executive and to watch him with the customers was a real experience. We spent many meetings in which we were required to negotiate price and share. He would also invite me and my spouse over to dinner or he and I would just play golf. There were many golf experiences with customers even though I still wasn't that good; however, I just focused on having a good time because customers hated seeing someone blow up over a golf match. I enjoyed my experiences with him as he was an excellent mentor who never blamed me for a share loss. He would focus on the reason we lost or gained share.

The position required a lot of customer visits reviewing their businesses and what we could do to support it. We usually had quite a cross function of the business discussing the issues. After the meetings it would be dinner and drinks. I was always picking up the bills. At one of the companies, the guys always wanted to go to the strip club after dinner. It was a lot of male bonding and they usually had a blast. One trip lasted well into the night, and we went around the back to see if any of the dancers wanted to go out. We didn't make it as the deputy sheriff said, "Boys, it's been quite a night and time to go home." We took his advice. One of the dilemmas from this was that I wound up with the dinner bill and the entertainment bill. I didn't want to have to answer a lot of questions about the bill or make up some funky labeling on the expense report as it probably would not have passed the newspaper test (how would it look in print). So I decided to pay these bills personally.

It was a tough two years, but I made a lot of friends who were constantly giving me feedback and support. At the end of two years, the finance organization wanted me to go back into finance. The company was trying to broaden business leaders and then getting them back into their original functions. So I went back into Finance Manager of the aircraft engines production division.

CHAPTER 10

Aircraft Engines

The production division encompassed manufacturing, quality, and engineering functions comprising roughly seventeen thousand employees in twelve locations. In addition, I also served on the board of directors of three joint ventures the largest of which was Famat in France, who had an agreement with GE to share in the manufacture of engines for the 737 aircraft. I sat on the Boards of the JV in Turkey, Famat and CFAN.

    The position required me to support two different business leaders at the same time, the vice president of manufacturing, Chuck who couldn't have been more professional, thoughtful, smart, and committed. He was someone that you always wanted to support. I was constantly looking at his leadership style and trying to learn. He could have cared less what the CFO, Bill was saying. Bill was a powder keg always ready to explode; personally, I was one of the few people that could understand what drove him. An example would be that he and I would work up an operating plan that the organization could commit to and then he would rant and rave about some poor chauffeur who was still in the budget (as I liked to say, a pimple on the elephant's butt). The production division had a chauffeur to take customers back and forth to the Airport; however, it drove the CFO nuts.

Every staff meeting, monthly estimates, inventory plan reviews, were brutal and constantly putting me between the two business leaders. I participated in all budget meetings and staff meetings, and if I was not adding value, then I wouldn't have been invited. Along with Chuck's staff, we would put together a budget with a lot of "stretch" (reduced costs or lower inventories). We would then review it with the VP of manufacturing. When it was completed, I then took it to the VP of finance. It was never good enough and needed more "stretch" less costs, lower inventory, lower headcount, etc.

This was hard because I knew how much reductions were already in the plan; however, it was never enough, and then Bill would then add more. I would then have to take it back to manufacturing where we would then go back and forth until everyone agreed and committed to the reductions and the budget. I used to dread these discussions and confrontations because it took so much of my and others time, and yes, the chauffer was still in the budget. I spent two years watching and learning the leadership styles of both of these VPs. I took the best traits from both (and there were many traits from both individuals) and threw the bad styles in the trash.

Part of this new position was an annual physical by the businesses doctor. Our doctor whose name was Dr. Zerbe was a very good doctor with a great sense of humor. He would give me my physical including stress test and bloodwork and then wait for the results. He would then call you back in and go over what he found. One of the big things with my physical was my liver functions were really elevated. He asked me if I knew of any reason and I said no.

He then asked me how many drinks of alcohol I had a night. At first I said two. He then said, "Let me ask this again. How many drinks do you have?" I then said maybe three. He then asked me again, and I said four. He then explained that I had to cut down on my drinking as eventually I would have severe problems with my liver. I thanked him and waited for my next year's physical where we went through the same discussions. Fortunately, these physicals were for the individual and not shared with the company. Although, I did hear something funny later on in my career. The story goes that Jack was discussing something with the companies doctor and commented that 60 percent of his executives were on Prozax and the other 40 percent didn't know that they should be. I don't know if it was true but it was really funny.

I loved the business, seeing these huge aircraft engines being built on the line and then on to quality to test them. For instance, the many ways aircraft engines were tested was to perform the bird test. To perform this situation, they would throw a twelve-pound bird into the blades to simulate a bird strike. The environmental persons had a field day with this and demanded that we do something about it. The outcome was that we would throw defrosted turkeys into the blades for the test. It wasn't the same but worked. At the end of each month, there were always a few engines that didn't ship because of FOB (foreign object damage). Inevitably, someone would leave a ladder or large tools in the test chamber and it would get sucked through the engine. You just prayed it wasn't an employee which had happened before.

We planned a visit to Famat and the joint venture we had with them on the GE 737 engine. Going over, we had to travel coach and the plane was absolutely packed. We were in the last row near the bathroom, which flushed all night long. My traveling partner was the engineer and he kept ordering vodka drinks. Well, halfway through dinner, he throws up in his napkin. He blamed it on the food. So now I had to deal with the coach seating, the bathroom and the smell of puke. I was unable to get any sleep, and it was a terrible flight. I arrived the next day, certainly not on my game.

We had a factory tour where they built the engines and then we did the board meeting. The next day, we traveled to the JV factory. It was located in the northwest corner of France. It was a nice factory and production was good. We had our business meeting and tour and there wasn't anything that appeared out of line. I found out that the beaches there were topless which, I just had to visit. It was a cool day and there were few people on the beach. We traveled back to Famat's headquarters and factory to pay our respects before we traveled home.

We developed a joint venture, which we called CFAN. The JV was to develop the fan blades for the GE 90 Engines that we were trying to build so the blades were absolutely a critical part. This engine would be the latest technology to power the 787 aircraft, which could handle many more passengers and travel further than any plane in the current fleets. It was a new design and they were having problems in developing the blades. We kept working to develop the blades as it was critical to the development timeline. Chuck and I made a visit to the JV to look at the organization, progress, plans, and determine what if anything needed changing or what from headquarters we could assist in. It was extremely fascinating to look at the process and how big those blades were. We were then given a factory tour and after that, we spent the afternoon going through the manufacturing progress, projects, and ideas on successfully developing the blades.

I visited our factory in Turkey (Board meeting). To get there, you had to drive about an hour and a half down the highway of death. It was named this because it was a two lane highway and people were constantly passing. Unfortunately, they didn't care about cars coming the other way and there were numerous head on collisions. All along the way there were just wrecked cars along the side of the highway. We made it to the factory and held the business review and factory tour. Turkey was a key customer and a strategic partner not only for us but also the country itself. The souvenirs from Turkey were casted jet planes (copper alloy). I bought an F-16 fighter and a lot of beautiful Meerschaum pipes. I always tried to shop in every country I visited.

On another time, I was working late into the night and when I left, the gates were barricaded and they were operated by military police. I was motioned to stop my car and show my ID. It turned out that it was the beginning of the first Gulf War. It made it clear what we're producing was important to the country.

Bill had built a world-class financial team, which included the CFOs for sales finance, Keith, myself, and the CFO of military engines all of whom were high potential individuals.

Corporate was looking to him for candidates and he recommended both Keith and myself. Corporate thought that I didn't have the experience to do the job and wasn't ready. He pushed back and thought that I was an excellent candidate. If not for his insistence that I was ready, I would never have been on the slate to interview. So the CFO that I was constantly butting heads with became my biggest supporter. The position was chief financial officer of GE transportation run by a business leader (Bob) that was in the running for replacing Jack Welch the outcome of the interviews was that one of us would get transportation and the other individual would go to Bergan Op Zum in the Netherlands (Plastics).

I noticed that the CEO kept a picture of his daughter on his desk. She was at the beach in her bikini. I thought it was a test whether you maintained eye contact with him or stared at the picture. We both interviewed well and the deciding factor was my background in sales. I went to Transportation.

The reality of events that resulted in my becoming CFO of one of the thirteen businesses: (1) mentorship by key executives, (2) networking both up and down, (3) getting candid insights and looking for ways to improve, (4) the ability to deal with surprises in a professional way, (5) technical skills to do the job, (6) having cross functional experience and (7) having the integrity to do things right both in GE and out.

CHAPTER 11

The Eddie Russell Affair

Before I go into my experience at Transportation, one of the bizarre events that happened while I was at aircraft engines was when I came back to my office from lunch one day and I saw a phone message from the CFO of plastics, Bob (I recognized the area code). I called him back and he asked me if I was sitting down. He informed me that Ed Russel (my CEO at Superabrasives) had filed a lawsuit against GE and alleged unfair dismissal, issues with the handling of the tax issue at diamonds, that I had paid a bribe in Europe and had signed off on expense accounts that included prostitutes and other charges.

These were just a few of the issues in the lawsuit but those I was intimately familiar with. You could've heard a pin drop. I was shaking so bad, it's like being charged with sexual harassment, how do you defend yourself? I knew that the allegations were bogus and had no basis in fact. The CFO of Plastics told me that if I wanted to have a lawyer to represent me personally (versus the company lawyers), that the company would pay the cost provided that I was not guilty. I declined the offer of legal counsel because

I had done nothing wrong. (One of the biggest mistakes of my career.)

He also informed me that at this time, there were already audits taking place in Superabrasives to review transactions and hold meetings with key personnel. Remember that I was Ed's CFO for seven months. What I understood had happened was he gave too many wrong answers to the questions being asked by Jack Welch. At business meetings everyone who was ever going to pitch to Jack better know their facts. The worst thing that you could do was to make something up to one of his questions. Jack knew the business operations and markets of every business. He had an incredible knowledge and remembered everything from prior pitches. Each business had three planned presentations and they were all pretty intense.

The three reviews were (session 2), which covered a midyear performance to the business plan (budget) and outlook for the remaining year. Session 1, which was an outlook for five years on new products, services, market, and competitors and any other threat or opportunities that may happen to the products or markets. In addition he reviewed technology and of course the five-year outlook on financials. And the last was session C, which was a human resources review of all the individuals on their ranking, coding, and peer reviews of key personnel. I always stayed up late prior to presentations to review my pages and anticipate questions which might be asked. I always felt intense about the reviews (and a little worried) that I would do a good job. So Ed Russell was supposedly winging responses to questions and he was told to go back to get the market data and facts and then meet again. Also at this time, he was in and all-out war with his CFO slinging shit all over each other.

This was never a good situation and quite frankly just plain stupid on both parts. Unfortunately, the answers at the meeting were still unsatisfactory and Jack was tired of the responses and fired Ed. The reason for my involvement was that I was the CFO of Superabrasives, when he was named as the president and CEO of the business. Ed and I got along together during my tenure. He actually had spent time understanding the production side of the business. In fact at times, I felt that he was down in the minutia. I was just not sure he completely understood the sales opportunities with new and evolving products and markets.

He wanted badly to be considered part of the group of employees who partied on weekends (he was in the process of an ugly divorce). It was bad enough that he was chasing the crowd and going out with the group to drink and dance. Picture a forty-year-old man doing break dancing and chasing a partying group of employees. For those of you who feel that what happens on weekends should be your business, remember that you were required to represent the company at all the times, twenty-four hours a day, seven days a week. If that was a problem then you were with the wrong company. When I left Superabrasives, one of my closest friends was named CFO.

Unfortunately, he did not get along (at all) with Ed. He would talk to me about the issues of items that they disagreed on and the person that he was pursuing (trying to date). Every week, there would be a new problem between them it just kept going with no end in sight. I gave him some advice, which did not change the acrimony between them. I told him that making this public in the company would be a career ending move and to try to find some common ground to do his job with Ed. They just were constantly throwing shit on each other and in the end nobody won. In addition, the situation was slowly working up the leadership of GE. So at the end of the day, Ed was terminated and married the individual who he was pursuing, and the CFO left the company.

So back to the lawsuit, he threw mud at everybody, Jack, Dennis, Bob, and me along with others. The huge number of people and time to review every allegation took an enormous amount of energy and time not to mention costs. On a personal standpoint, the audit staff had determined that I had not paid a bribe oversees and I didn't sign off on any expense accounts containing prostitutes. The bribe he claimed that I made was from our German office, which I visited frequently. The CFO, Werner, of this operation was top notch and helped me understand the European business. He was a solid manager of finance and there would be no way that he would let a bribe be paid on his watch.

Every individual named in the lawsuit had to go through the review process. Remember that I declined a personal attorney. On the day of my deposition, the company had their lawyer attend. We had lunch before the deposition and talked about what may come up. The deposition began and immediately got ugly. The questions started on my involvement in the transfer pricing issue that had been cleared up. They were very detailed questions and just continued on every element of the review. I turned to the Company attorney and asked if I had to respond to these questions.

He informed me that it was their deposition and they could ask anything they wanted. I did not know this. I thought that they could only ask questions about the allegations to me. This went on for a couple of hours, they claimed that Dennis had hid the events and did not report it to the taxing authorities. Obviously this was not true, but it was more shit that he could make up and created havoc trying to resolve, each claim had to be reviewed to determine if they were true or false. After three hours of these questions, I asked for a break to use the facilities. So there I was using the urinal when Ed Russell walked in and took the urinal next to me. (There were ten empty urinals.) He asked me how I was doing, how was my career, how was my family and that after all this was over maybe we could all go to dinner together.

I was in shock. My response was you have to be kidding me, all this crap you put me through and you want to go to dinner? The nerve of this guy even thinking that I would consider dinner was absurd. I did ask him why he was here today and he responded that he had nothing better to do and attended all the depositions. Another thing that I did not know could happen. The deposition continued to the pertinent issues and lasted another three hours. They would ask a question, I would respond and then they would slide a document over and ask me if wrote this.

LESSONS OF EXPERIENCE

One of the pertinent documents was the letter to the sales manager stating that he must state the reason for the dinner and in the future all items had to be explained completely and substantiated with receipts or the item would not be reimbursed. Although I felt they were excessive, I had no basis to determine that they were not for proper business. When we had finished and the corporate lawyer indicated that I did fine on all my responses. Late that day, he reported back to the company that I did very well and that the allegations were a figment of Ed's imagination. After millions of dollars and an unbelievable amount of peoples' time reviewing documents and conducting interviews to defend the suit, Ed accepted a settlement right before the trial was to begin. I thought of all the sleepless nights worrying what would happen and the enormous cost the company had expended. I wanted my day in court to prove my innocence which was naive.

Months later, I was pitching to Jack and he asked me about Ed and how I got along with him. I responded that after I had left he became delusional and was not the individual that I had worked for. Jack threw his hands in the air and said to the rest of the staff see there "I told you he was crazy." This ended the Eddie Russell affair. Lesson learned; if you ever have allegations about the financials, business practices, or sexual harassment allegations and you're offered a lawyer to represent you, don't be stupid enough not to accept. This lawsuit took a personal toll on every one as it took a tremendous amount of effort to review each individual allegation. There wasn't a day that I didn't think about the situation.

I absolutely knew I didn't do anything wrong but would there be a smoking gun out there in all those thousands of documents that would make me look bad? From this I learned not to keep a bunch of old letters, e-mails, business plans beyond the required retention time to comply with taxes. Otherwise, you might be defending every little detail. Make sure your company has a retention period on documents, email, and that everyone follows it to the letter!

CHAPTER 12

Six Sigma

We had been using "Work-out" for a number of years attacking all forms of productivity. We used "Work-out" for manufacturing improvements, process improvements, eliminating useless reports, reducing inventories, and eliminating all forms of waste. Every employee in the company was engaged. This included the hourly, non-exempt, salaried and executives. No good idea was turned away. As Jack put it "why pay for just the body when you can get the body and brains of every individual" "Work-out" was a huge success and significantly reduced costs and inventories. Subsequently, Jack had heard about a program being used by Motorola called Six Sigma and asked the Aircraft Engines finance team to go and find out what it entailed.

We spent the day understanding what the program was and listening to how it impacted their business. For the most part, I felt it was a hell of a process when it pertained to manufacturing or engineering for quality. I remember the person that was using it on journal entries. She gave a presentation on how it pertained to accounting operations specifically journal entries. She was concerned that if any of the entries were incorrect that it would take that many more correct entries to get back to Six Sigma.

She explained how the program had impacted their accounting processes and I just felt that it was a waste of time in this application. Coming home on the plane, we had taken a GE jet, we discussed their program and how, if any, it could help aircraft engines and the corporation. A lot of it was really good and was data focused. However some of it seemed like overkill. One of my takeaways was that it was data driven and you went where the data took you. I can remember thousands of meetings where someone would have an issue and I would immediately say it's probably because of this (no data, just gut feel). As with any major initiative, you have to tailor the initiative to your business.

A few of us felt that using Six Sigma for journal entries was taking it a little bit too seriously. However, we all knew of processes that if reviewed utilizing this methodology would make the process better and save money. It was presented at the following quarterly business review and there were a lot of questions. Jack was extremely interested in the program and challenged the business leaders to use it in their operations. The initiative was born that would have a lasting impact on GE and train the entire corporation into certified greenbelts and black belts. Six Sigma is a methodology used to improve business processes by using statistical analysis rather than guesswork.

It is a disciplined, data-driven approach, and methodology for eliminating defects (driving toward six standard deviations between the means and recent specification limit), in any process for all functions and businesses. It would develop techniques intended to improve processes by greatly reducing the probability that an error or defect would occur. Everyone was challenged to become certified as a greenbelt. Individuals would take the class and present a project within their business. Completion of the course and your project would qualify you to be a greenbelt. One could lead multiple projects over time and could become a black belt. Six Sigma was still being reviewed in detail at all business reviews with the edict that everyone must be Six Sigma certified by the end of the year otherwise no bonus.

All of a sudden, the classes were filled with executives attempting to get their certification. Every business would review their Six Sigma projects (it quickly became an I have more projects and higher cost reduction) in their business and the projected savings. Overnight, the businesses became process oriented; individuals that had Six Sigma qualifications were getting the promotions. Driving forward, Six Sigma was to become the most successful business initiative introduced in GE. The impact was a real game changer not only to operations but to the business leaders approach to solving problems. It was also determined that if you saw a good process somewhere else, it was okay to steal it. Not everything had to be your idea.

CHAPTER 13

From Planes to Trains

I began my CFO role at GE transportation a $1.4 billion dollar business that had around four thousand people in manufacturing and sales/service. Who wouldn't be excited about a business that built locomotives? Every person has saw or played with a train set in their lifetime. I spent the first three months learning all I could about the business. The CEO, Bob had a winning personality, he was bright and perceptive, and he was attempting to change the locomotive business from DC to AC locomotives. My job was to build a world-class financial team, to participate in sales operations going to customers with marketing and sales personnel, lead business development opportunities, and ensure the business hit their quarterly commitments.

It was the first CFO job that required me to lead in the development of an operations review. Usually, everyone would be working toward an operating plan that was presented to Jack and his staff in the September/October time period. There was also a five year outlook on the business, which included marketing, sales, manufacturing, business development, technology, and financials, which was completed in the May/June time frame. All thirteen manufacturing businesses as well as GE Capital were reviewed on each of these two meetings. We probably spent close to a month putting all the data into a cohesive business plan. The previous CFO that I replaced was a real numbers guy. He would take with him large notebooks of data. Just in case Jack asked a question.

I was responsible for the financial section of the presentation and cribbed my pages with notes that I thought were pertinent. The CEO didn't care which style you used as long as you could present your section of the presentation and answer any questions. We would spend a large amount of time practicing to ensure that the presentation was cohesive and that each leader knew what his commitment was and what he wanted his messages to be. The evening before the presentation, we would generally go up the day before and have dinner. On the way up, the sales manager kept asking me test questions to see how fast I could respond. Then the manufacturing leader asked me the square root of 3. I hesitated, he then said too late. This was giving me unwanted feedback at this point; all they were doing was busting my balls as the new guy. The CEO was nervous because I didn't take huge volumes of data with me.

The presentation went fine and my boss told me that I did a great job. We returned unscathed and now was the hard part, hitting every number and commitment that we made.

The CEO was a great mentor of mine. He allowed me to go on sales calls trying to convert railroads from DC to AC demonstrating the cost savings and payback of the move. We also thought there might be a service business if we could convince the railroads of the overall savings by either converting to AC or to letting us take over their service business. It turned out that the foreign countries were a perfect example. We made several trips to India to attempt to change their old DC locomotives with the AC or to let us manage all their DC locomotives with service shops.

Sales calls and business development was fun and my previous position in sales helped me immensely. There was a pitch that I created to show the Railroads positive cash flow detail. It was a huge development for me and I got to see most of the locomotive customers. We also made various international calls. We focused on India as they had a huge opportunity to convert their systems. It was felt that if we could get new locomotives there it was a big opportunity for service revenue.

The CEO and I pitch both concepts as well as a joint venture to the head of the Railways. Somewhere along the way of the discussion, it became obvious that there was something wrong with the financials. I noticed an error (in currency exchange) which dramatically changed the outcome, and it was in their favor. I corrected the problem and it was still a good return for both parties but the CEO was embarrassed. We left the meeting and he indicated that I could find my own way back home. We were traveling by corporate jet and he stayed mad as he indicated that I was on my own to get back to Erie, Pennsylvania. So I decided to stay working with the service personnel to refine the financials. It was still a good deal too both parties and it was supported by headquarters. Now I could go home.

India was amazing. Everyone in the businesses and hotels in remote locations left the windows open. This meant that you always had something flying or coming through the windows. The birds were okay but the monkeys were a problem. The little buggers would steal everything. It was bad karma to hurt any living creature so the people just learned to live with it. Once when I was in the south of India, I went to dinner; unfortunately I forgot to shut my suitcase. When I returned, my belongings where everywhere and the monkeys took anything that was shiny. You learn quickly to adapt. You also developed empathy for other human conditions. While looking out the window of my four star motel, I saw a construction site. The children were carrying rocks and small boulders out of the site and for this; they would get about $1/day if they were lucky. It was like slave labor, and it was amazing that they made due with the life that they had been dealt.

The CEO and I also went on a fact-finding mission to China to see if there were any business development opportunities (manufacturing, service, technology). We were given a presentation and then took a tour of a very large service building. There was lots of empty space. We rounded a corner and there was a couple having sex in the factory. I hated to think of what would happen to them. We had the usual ceremonial dinner and then came home. It was a good trip and we saw a lot of interesting things but the political climate would be difficult to overcome. It was up to me to follow up on everything.

I also worked with the Germans on the people moving business. These were the trams or small trains that moved people through airports or other large entities that needed trams or moving walkways. We focused on one airport and did a deep dive taking several months to work through all the details but the profit of a joint venture wasn't enough for us to move forward. It would be difficult to replace the existing people movers with new equipment so the revenues would have to rely heavily on the service business.

All of these business development projects took a lot of time and effort. Fortunately, I had an outstanding finance organization that could give me the time to work on the business.

The leadership team at Erie was a very helpful group of leaders that communicated well with all the sections of the business. They also were good mentors. I appreciated their constructive criticism. My experience of working with the team was not only helpful but was open enough to ensure they knew we were either on the upside or behind our business commitments. One of the other things I encountered was the Sharpie. Jack had not learned the usage of e-mail so when he had something to communicate, it came across the fax machine with a subject from Jack to the CEO and or the business teams; I just knew when a fax came in written with a Sharpie my life would get more interesting.

If there was any chance of not making your financials then you better be giving a heads up to Jack's vice president of Financial Analysis and Planning (FP&A), Bob. They would then look around for some other businesses to increase their commitment. To surprise Bob and therefore

Dennis was suicide because no one wants to be surprised, and then there was the possibility of not being able to get another business to pick up the slack. This was always an issue in that you want to support your CEO of the business and let him communicate to Jack before I communicated to Bob and eventually Dennis Dammerman.

To not communicate a miss was like putting your balls on the table to be whacked. This was the most important issue to manage. It was always a balancing match as no one wanted to communicate a miss. You would try every opportunity to see if you could cover the miss internally before you communicated upward. By the time you tried everything, it was too late. So you had the issue of not communicating in a timely manner. Enough of these and you would be considered unreliable. The corporation was known for hitting their commitments to the penny per share or slightly over.

During my time at Transportation, I hired a married couple to work for me. I needed someone to be the financial analyst and also a business development person to go to Asia. The CEO kept prodding me to get with the program as he thought I was moving to slow. He fully supported the couple and wanted it done right away. So I offered them the job(s). As soon as Dennis became aware of it he called me and proceeded to rip my ass, among other things, it was brutal to say nothing. I was being ripped to shreds and I was sure that I was going to be fired. When he was all done, I was finally able to say two words.

I apologized for my ignorance of the process to promote someone overseas and it would not happen again.

He then asked how I was doing and how was the family and if there was anything I needed. He had made his point emphatically and there was no reason to fester on it. You knew what you had to do. I informed the couple that they would not be going to Asia and that only Dennis could approve it and he wasn't going to.

Transportation was a big industry in Erie. Housing was very difficult especially for somebody looking for a mother-in-law suit. I wound up having to build. There was a lot next to me that was also beginning construction. In the fall and winter, I could see lake Erie. The house was completed and my Family moved from Cincy. I had been living in temporary housing until the house was finished. My next-door neighbor moved in a couple of months later and coming back from church on Sunday, there was a red Mercedes in my driveway. It turned out that he owned the Mercedes dealership and said that no neighbor of his could drive anything else.

He said to drive it around for a few days and that he would give me a good deal. I declined to keep it. He was a little miffed so a couple of weeks later I asked him for the same car in black. I wound up buying the car, however, parking it in my reserved space at work caused a reaction from the union that business must be good (for the executives). You can never win. However, it emphasized the impact that some of your personal decisions could have on the business.

One of the rewards for an executive was the annual business meeting every January. It was held in the Boca Raton Golf and Country Club and was always first class.

I would usually be vacationing in Florida with my parents and Bob would usually stop to pick me up in Clearwater as it was on the way to Boca. The first thing was getting a room at the main building. Usually the first timers went across the bay bridge and it was always difficult to change clothes for golf and other activities. The mornings were filled with presentations from selected business leaders that Jack wanted to show the executives a new idea, process or new sales initiative. The afternoons were filled with golf, sport fishing, or guided tours.

You were able to select your individual activity. I always chose golf as I was actually getting better at it and the activity was handicapped. You had to have a handicap that was attested to in order to limit the amount of people who would cheat on their handicaps. The golf was always a blast and you met a lot of new people to network with.

During our afternoon of golf, Jack would always go ahead so that he didn't run into anybody as he played extremely fast with a select foursome of executives that were equally good. Well on this day, he bumped into us. We were all waiting on the seventeenth hole as the course had become backed up. I offered that they could play through but he declined. My worst nightmare was holding Jack up my next nightmare was having him watch me hit a shot. We all teed off and luckily I hit it just on the green, it was a Par three. We then stepped off the green and let them play through. I was extremely happy that I had hit the green so that I didn't look like a hack.

In the evening, we had dinner with different business leaders. They always mixed up the people at tables so that you had a chance to meet someone new. The dinners were always excellent and then the evening was free. I heard that there were some high stake poker games with the bids sometimes in the thousand-dollar range. It was too rich for my blood. Usually, I would go offsite with some friends or just go back to my room.

On one meeting, two of the senior members of the finance team wanted me to go with them to a strip club. We loaded into a Limo and watched the girls dancing and participated in some lap dances. We had some drinks but nobody got really loaded and then we piled back into the Limo and headed back. The whole time, I felt like I was being tested to determine if I was a congenial part of the group and what my reactions would be to the trip. I had a good time and didn't really care; besides, I had made some really good friends.

One of the things that always made me nervous was being a speaker at Boca. You had around a half hour to give your business topic and about a month to develop your presentation. Usually, the speakers did really well and the audience was always impressed. The thought though of standing up in front of my peers made me extremely nervous. Fortunately, I was never chosen to speak. I really always got a lot out these meetings and would go back and summarize them so that I could inform my staff of any new initiatives.

CHAPTER 14

Developing GE leaders

The company used three executive classes to evaluate high potential candidates. There was the Management Development Course (MDC), Business Management Course (BMC), and the Executive Development Course (EDC). Each year, the businesses would recommend individuals for these programs. The recommendations came from every function. You had to be a high potential to attend the classes. They were attended in the appropriate time in your career and based on your appraisals and coding. If you wanted to continue to get ahead you had to have outstanding performance and peer reviews.

The courses were taught in a private setting located in Crotonville, New York. It is set up like a sprawling campus with an education center, dorm rooms, and offices/dinner facility. My first trip there the dorm rooms were like college with several persons sharing a room. Later, the facility was completely remodeled so that each individual had a private room which was more conducive to sleeping and studying. The facility was operated by an outside hotel staff. The education center held a main auditorium and conference rooms for break out meetings.

The best and well known educators taught from many different US Universities. It was also staffed with professional educators/training staff that monitored students in a variety of settings and gave their evaluations of the individuals. You were able to return home in the middle of the class which left two weekends for education, studying or an outside activity. Depending on the time of the year, we would always try to catch a Yankees game. The experience left you with a variety of friends that you could network with for the balance of your career.

I went to MDC when I was the CFO for Superabrasives. Every executive class was one month in duration. This particular class had a one week module on finance to non-financial individuals. Every program included individuals from manufacturing, engineering, sales, HR, and finance. The remainder of the class was teaching modules that could help you understand the company. There was always a cocktail hour so that the individuals could meet the other people in the class. You did not want to have too much to drink at any of these courses. The training staff was constantly reviewing each individual and their performance not only in the classes but at all breaks and social events (cocktail hour and dinner). You hoped that you stood out enough to be leaving a favorable impression.

I was sent to the Business Management Course (BMC) in 1989 when I was the manager heating and air-conditioning sales operations. This class was on the road for three weeks except with the last week to prepare and present your findings. We were charged to find developing businesses to partner with GE. The class was to go out and find excellent businesses and opportunities in the Far East. I was fortunate enough to form a team with two others to look at China. Other members of the class choose other countries. Every country and business that we visited we were treated first class. We arrived in China on Thursday or Friday. We were staying at the Hilton in Shanghai.

This was during the Tiananmen protests. We each had someone in the government that watched our every move. I had some fun with mine as I would open my door to go out and then shut it real quick, it was funny to watch as he flew out of his room to find me looking right and left. I had also got dressed to go running. I headed down the road (I thought if I just went straight I couldn't get lost). I turned to come back to the hotel only to suddenly realize that I felt that I was lost. I've had these feelings before and usually was okay so I tried to ignore my initial fears. Well, the longer I ran, it became apparent that I was really lost with no idea how to get back. I kept asking people if they knew where the Shilton was (the Hilton's name in China). I walked around doing this until the police showed up to take me back to the hotel. Thank goodness I had a shadow.

Everybody was on edge that night given the events that were happening in Beijing. The next day we were given a tour of a palace to shop for gifts. Leaving the shopping area our translator indicated that we had just spent more on gifts than what an ordinary person would make all year. It didn't matter whether you were a doctor or a street cleaner; everybody got paid the same amount. Any excess in your pay went to the Chinese government and as we were walking around, I commented on how many people were coming into the city on bikes or buses. I was getting uncomfortable given the circumstances.

I mentioned that it looked like the city would fall the next day. We went out to dinner with a company and government officials that night. They had a wonderful dinner and had what they considered cuisine to honor their guests from America. In the middle of the table was a large raw fish and everyone used chopsticks to take little blocks of the fish. We had been eating the fish for a while when I reached for a piece of fish, and the fish jumped off the serving platter. It kept flopping around on the table until they got it back on the platter. I immediately did a George Bush and went to the bathroom and threw up. I went back to the table feeling better and only ate cooked items.

Sure enough, we woke the next day with a city in revolt. Buses were burning or overturned, items were burning all over the place, people blocking streets and everything that could be burned or torn apart was. We were told to pack our bags as quickly as we could to go to the airport; the city had become a risk to visitors. We got in our minivan to go to the Airport. It was near impossible to go down a street without something blocking your way. There were over turned barrels, cars, and busses. You would start to go down a little road and would have to go another way to the airport or trying to get by the protesters and again turn around and take another road.

This took a long time to finally get to the airport. We were in a hurry because a commercial plane had been waiting on the tarmac for us this entire time. When we got there, the baggage handler would not accept our bags. There was a fist fight between our driver and the baggage handler. It lasted briefly and our luggage was taken to the plane. The three of us got on the plane and it immediately took off. It was the last plane to leave the airport. The plane took us to Singapore where we decided to finish our project in Taiwan. From there, we had set up visits to other companies to determine opportunities in this region. The entire review lasted about two weeks and then we were given about three or four days to develop presentations on our findings to executives and business management.

I volunteered to give the presentation putting aside my fear of public speaking. I didn't know why I felt that way as I had always been given compliments whenever I gave a presentation. Paolo Fresco (a co-chairman) was the highest executive in the room along with other regional executives. The presentation included the company's we visited and the risk and reward of using them. Our conclusion was to not invest in China as it was just too risky at this time. Without the right environment, we would be down the road for three to five years and then some political event would take place and change the whole opportunity. It was an interesting global experience. It was always positive working with your classmates who were also high potentials representing their businesses.

The last class was an Executive Development Class (EDC) this was the class that molds you for the future. I attended when I was with Nuovo, Pignone in Italy. The CFO, human resources, and legal reported to me. My title was "Generali Manager of Generali Affairs" (general manager of General Affairs). We did not get rid of the current CFO because we were afraid that it would create too much upheaval for the Italian government and that his knowledge about the business would leave too much of a void. The EDC class specialized in leadership programs, how to deal with the public, public speaking and proper etiquette. I like to call it finishing school.

It also included presentations by corporate staff including company financials and current initiatives. Jack, as he had always done, visited us and gave us an update of GE along with taking questions. We were given projects on business issues which contain five to ten people on each team. We would research the issue and possible outcomes to various GE businesses. We would then develop a presentation on the subject to give at the GE officers meeting. Another individual wanted to present our findings and conclusions. I let him do it which was a big mistake because the individual that presented got all the exposure to the officers. They remembered the presenter and not necessarily the rest of the team. As always, you were evaluated by the onsite staff (your participation with your peers analyzing the issue and putting the project into presentation form). This was the class to identify individuals to be elected officers of the company. As usual, we all went back to our businesses with renewed energy.

CHAPTER 15

Nuovo Pignone, Italy

I walked up to Dennis during a Christmas party for the CFOs and Corporate Finance Staff. This was an annual event which included spouses and everybody looked forward to the evening. He asked me what I thought about Florence. I responded that we didn't own anything in Florence, Kentucky. He looked at me and said you really are in need of some culture. He was talking about Florence, Italy. Specifically a business that we just bought called Nuovo Pignone a $1.6 billion-dollar sales operation at eight manufacturing locations and employing around five thousand people. We talked for a while and I told him I would talk to my wife.

Following that discussion I told him that I would be interested in the position. I had two interviews the first with his vice president of international finance Alberto and provided that that went well, I would interview with Paolo Fresco who was a co-chairman responsible for all operations internationally. I didn't have to interview with the CEO of Power Systems because everyone knew that Bob was going to become the new CEO of Power Systems. I must've done well with the interviews because the next thing I knew I was wrapping up my US possessions. This required us to sell both cars and anything else not going into storage. My wife was really excited about the move and could not stop telling everybody about the opportunity.

We wrapped up what we had to do and were all set to travel to Italy. One issue settled around how to get the dog to Florence. Nike was a beautiful Champion French bulldog who I couldn't get rid of. The airlines would handle the flights from JFK to Brussels and then to Rome so the only trip that was left uncovered was the Erie, Pa, to JFK. It turns out that I was approved to use the corporate jet from Erie to JFK. It was probably the first time that any dog traveled in Jack's plane. I prayed that she didn't have to go to the bathroom or got sick on the flight. The kids loved the private jet and thought that the upper deck of a 747 and business class was great. Once there, we cleared immigration and the baggage handlers were playing with the dog. She had a great personality and loved to play with anybody.

It was a miracle that I was able to get up to speed at the business so quickly and still manage the home front and visa issues. When I had left the US, I was assured we would not have any meetings with Jack to review the financials for at least three months so that I could come up to speed and get settled; however, Jack wanted to know the financials of the business after one month so much for assurances.

Our CEO was a boisterous man who was quick to make everyone comfortable. He knew four Italian words *boun giorno* and *bouno notte*, which meant good morning and good night. He quickly made the business relax. He spent his time coming up to speed on the business production, technology, and sales. He had the comfort of having the previous CEO of this business who was now the honorary chairman and the vice president of Production and Engineering. The business knew two measurements which were sales and employment. As long as both were increasing the business was a success to them. The last one was to not pay taxes to the government.

Of course, these were not the measurements of a GE acquisition. Rising sales would be a good measure; however, we would like to see growing revenues and the same or decreased number of employees that would generate productivity and increased profitability. This was not good to the Italians as decreasing people was a real issue to them. I should note that no GE team that went in initially for any acquisition had ever succeeded. I was very lucky because I received a great person in the role of financial, planning, and analysis, Reno. He spoke fluent Italian and was a Godsend to me. We went to the business and put together a financial package. I also met with Alberto, who had responsibility for international finance. We worked a lot together, and he always gave me good advice. So we put together the initial presentation to Jack on the financials that we were able to put together and what our first impressions were of the business and what we would begin to change. The meeting was very successful and we all looked forward to seeing the business succeed.

So every morning, I would start off the day with my lessons to speak Italian and the rest of the day developing a world-class finance team along with continued efforts to put in measurements conducive to a GE business. There were continuous business reviews, and the Italians thought that all these presentations were crazy as they were being asked to put together metrics which they were responsible for. The other areas that we were trying to achieve were associated with GE culture and integrity. The presentations were becoming more and more frequent and were becoming more accurate. I should note that the business was a huge success and everybody wanted to be part of the transition. We were the shining gem in power systems which is where we reported. John's boss on a direct line was Bob (my previous CEO at Transportation) the new CEO for Power Systems and mine was Tom, the CFO I took over from at Transportation.

Bob had managed to put the two CFOs that he trusted the most into the roles. Everyone wanted to find a reason to visit the business. Our biggest challenge was to have fewer meetings so that we could get some work done. Also, the power systems business was struggling to hit their commitments as Power Generation was in a recession and so they were constantly asking us for more and more net income. This was highly visible to the Italians who didn't want the business to be raped. The CEO and I were constantly fighting the issue to give more net income until Paolo stepped in a said enough, leave the business be successful. The company also had the philosophy to change the culture of an acquisition as soon as possible. In this case, the culture was what made the business successful. We were of the opinion to go slowly on the culture change until we knew exactly what we were changing and why.

All the functions were constantly being reviewed by the Corporation. The Italians still didn't understand the constant presentations, but we were able to convince them about our culture and the number of presentations. Each year, the business became more recognized. They certainly did not agree on the presentations; however, they understood it. Everyone wanted to be part of the success. By this time, we continued to collect data and understand the processes which were necessary and important. We focused on the two major presentations, which were the status of the business plan, and preparing its five-year forecasts.

The house in Italy was pretty nice, close to the American school, but a pretty long ride to the headquarters. I was promised a driver for the first and second months, so that I could get acclimated to the business. GE did not want to let the current CFO leave before we could transfer information to me. As I noted earlier, my title was going to be general manager of General Affairs. We had a person in Milan that was handling our visas and arranging for housing and any other issues that came up. A few months later, we found out that my work visa did not go through and I had to leave the country for thirty days. I was not supposed to work in any part of Europe; however, I chose London to work from, because it's a nice city, I knew my way around. It was convenient to all of Europe, and the GE offices in London had all the technology and of course I could say I wasn't working.

My wife practically did nothing all day while I was working and didn't try to learn the language even though GE was providing lessons. In addition, the scorpions that she kept finding in the house freaked her out. To her, it was a third-world country (her words, not mine) after nine months; she had enough and wanted to return to the States. I felt that she never gave the country a chance. This was even after GE had approved Nicky for the kids and my wife. Pam could use her to drive around (she took the kids to school and picked them up), communicate, and fix dinners if needed.

The kids were acclimating great to the American school and to make sure everything was okay, I joined the Board of Directors of school. I used the Massimo my driver to only go to work, business dinners, and home. He was available all day for her if she wanted to go anywhere if Nicky was unavailable. I also bootlegged the English cable company so the kids had English TV. In addition, Nicky had moved into the downstairs room of the house (with her significant other) so she could help my wife with anything. We went to the markets on Saturday; you never knew what would be hanging from the rafters and the type of things in the refrigerated cases. In the case were cow brains, chickens with their feet and according to my youngest, dead birds (game birds and pheasants). After she left, the house was just too big for one person so I moved to a converted barn just up from Galileo's home.

It was a nice place with a living room, two bedrooms (one upstairs and one in the basement), and two baths. The company also decided that I could keep Nicky to clean and cook meals. We spent Saturdays just walking around Florence and visiting the tourists sites or visiting jewelers where I would add to my pocket watch collection. When it was time to go back to the house, I would visit a florist and buy enough flowers for the home for the next week. You walked everywhere in Florence as cars other than limo's or taxis were not allowed. The walking was good exercise in addition to the nightly runs I would take with Nicky to clear my mind. We usually went in town where we could run around the park.

We continued our efforts to implement the financial, production, engineering, and systems integration, along with business integration and a business culture that mirrored GE, to the extent possible. There were two major policies 20.4, which were business practices and policy 20.5 price-fixing. These two policies were sign by all US personnel in the company. They had no problem with the latter policy and agreed to sign it. Policy 20.4 was an overreaching understanding on the way we did business, which contain provisions about bribes. It had the provision that if you knew of someone violating the policy that you would turn them in. The business leaders felt that they could agree on the policy personally but turning people in was too much like World War II and they wouldn't sign.

I sat down with the operation leaders and ask them to help me out. They indicated that they could not sign anything that reminded them of Nazi collaboration. I thought about it for a while and concluded that if they would sign it for themselves that they would not violate the policy then in the end, it met the spirit of the policy. This was acceptable and everyone signed it.

One of John's and my favorite events was to eat at Harry's Bar, which was a little expensive but we loved the atmosphere of this restaurant. Not only did they prepare great food but the bar was fantastic. Well, we were sitting there one night and in walked Arnold Palmer I mentioned to John that Arnold Palmer had just walked in. He turned to look and he said that it wasn't him as he had golfed with Arnold. I keep saying, "Yes, it was." So John walked over to introduce himself.

He said my friend over there keeps saying that you are Arnold Palmer. He said that I was correct. John then introduced both of us, I asked what he was here for, and he said that he was reviewing some plans to build a golf course. I said glad to meet you and went back to my table. Surely he wanted the evening to look at the designs without being interrupted by two GE executives but he was very polite. Everything I had ever read was that he was one of the greats and a real gentleman.

Paolo was able to protect the business (our God Father) he decided he wanted to play a round of golf with me. I was worried about the real reason for the meeting. We did have access to the country club golf course, and he and I played the course. He was having trouble with everything he was hitting. Almost everything he hit dribbled up the fairway or went out of bounds. I was watching how he was doing and yelled out to keep your fucking head down. I immediately regretted having said that as it was both unprofessional and vulgar. I wasn't sure he was okay with the unsolicited advice.

But the glare was overwhelming as it lasted a few seconds more than normal. He focused the rest of the round playing with his head down and was pleased with the way he played. Of course he won the round. We then took a shower and had some late lunch. We talked about the business and how I was doing. All in all, I thought it was an enjoyable day. The purpose it turned out was to screen me as a candidate to be elected to the Board which I was subsequently named.

One of the major issues that hit the business was when I found out that the way they controlled cost was by having a separate warehouse containing inventory that was not on the books. This way if they had too much net income, they would scrap more parts into the warehouse and thus increasing costs and lowering net income to avoid paying taxes. The opposite was true if they didn't have enough net income then they would just take parts and enter them into production without any cost. Cleary this was a major problem. I communicated the issue first to the Alberto and Paolo.

I then informed Dennis. Everyone was concerned about the impacts not only to the financials but also to who knew what and when. We wanted to know the facts without creating a witch hunt. Everyone had their opinions as to how to handle the next steps. I suddenly became inundated with too much help. I didn't need the corporate audit staff to quantify the issue as everyone knew what the value was. What I needed was some good tax advice. The company had a really good vice president of Taxes Samuel and he was readily available to help.

Others had different ideas on what could be done. I was starting to receive too much help. I had the company Controller Phil, the company's treasurer Bob, the audit staff, and of course, Alberto. The company just wanted to ensure that I had all the facts and was right in the way I wanted to handle it and that there was no other options. At the end of the day it was I who had to sign off on the financial records and the easiest and correct way was to just move the inventory back on the books and thus increase our net income and taxes. The outcome of this was writing a very large check to the Italian government for taxes.

As I have alluded to, one of the biggest issues was too many visits. Everyone likes to be associated with a success. We were being inundated with presentations, factory tours, and dinners. It was becoming just too much to handle all the visits along with dinners, thankfully it settled down after the first year. However, we still had the presentations with Jack, Bob, and Paolo which kept us more than busy. It still drove the Italians nuts.

Other assignments that were given to me during my time at Nuovo Pignone was to operate the European Finance Council for all of the CFOs in Europe. The council exchanged ideas on cost savings and financial processes. We met every month to review the status of operating plans and Six Sigma projects and any other problems or opportunities. I enjoyed these meetings and we tried to pick a different location for every meeting. As such, I was able to see most of Europe.

LESSONS OF EXPERIENCE

In addition to these two jobs, I was asked to overview financials for power generation on all business quotes. The primary job here was to ensure that we had good margins on orders and that there wasn't any business practice violations or bribes. The latter was important because it was illegal. This would send the wrong message about our integrity and culture.

I visited Saudi Arabia GE sales office to meet with a big Power Generation customer. It took a day to learn some of the customs. For one, there were no female administration assistants. The women are not allowed to work. Alcohol of any type or nude magazines were forbidden. The entire staff lived in an offsite compound. The women were not allowed to drive. One of the most interesting events was the beheadings of convicted criminals every Friday in the town square at noon. I was curious about this but could not find anyone to go with me. We had the usual dinners and I learned that the women and children were not allowed to eat with the men in the main dining room.

Afterward, we went to the compound (for safety). There we could get a cocktail as the alcohol came through the diplomatic pouch and the compounds actions were not viewed by the Saudis. The next day, we visited the customer on a large deal. We went through our entire proposal along with the financials. Unfortunately, during the conversation they casually mentioned that the competition was offering some kickbacks (a bribe). I told the customer that we just couldn't do that (it was a multimillion dollar order). I felt we still had the best proposal. I told the BoB what had happened and he supported my position. We lost the sale, but we sent a message to the region that we could not operate like that. We still had a thriving business there based on value and price.

The orders in Europe that had paper thin margins were not consummated unless we could obtain some service business. I enjoyed the role immensely as I was able to travel around the Middle East and gain enough knowledge about the sales process.

It was a beautiful spring day, and I was awaiting the planned arrival of three of our board members. We gave them a small presentation of the business and then John had arranged that I take them on a tour of the factory and what we could do better. The tour lasted around and hour and I left them to freshen up before dinner. What John didn't understand was that they wanted to see him give the tour. We had dinner with the key executives and they left the next day. What nobody knew was they were here to get a better knowledge of John as his name had come up to replace Jack. That was a recommendation that could not be made. He left GE shortly after that to become a CEO of a public company. Shortly after he was on his new job I interviewed for his CFO position. Despite everything we had been through together I did not get the job because his staff felt we were too close and I wouldn't be objective enough.

I had brought together a lot of the European trained Six Sigma personnel from many of the businesses. The meeting was to hold a forum to review best practices and Six Sigma initiatives. I was the kick off speaker and I looked out and saw this very pretty woman in the front row. Unfortunately, she had three buttons undone of her blouse. It was to say the least distracting. It was hard to look at the rest of the crowd because I kept focusing on her.

All my trained Six Sigma personnel were there along with my staff. I was giving my presentation on best practices and every time I looked down she was right there and I could see the tops of her breasts. I was trying to give my presentation without any issues. I was getting close to the end and I was supposed to say best practices, but what I said was breast practices. I thought maybe it went unnoticed so I wrapped up my presentation and walked back to my staff. I asked them if I really said breast practices and they were rolling on the floor. That afternoon, I was hoping that my error would not create a problem or that I offended anyone. I always worried too much what people would think.

During my last year at the business two events took place. The business hired a new CEO to replace John. His name was Dennis, and he was and engineer by background. He was a pleasant man and we got along pretty well. He pushed back a lot on Power Systems and he got along great with the Italian leadership who were by background also engineers. Of course I had to spend a lot of time bringing him up to speed on the business but he was a fast learner who quickly gained a knowledge of the engineering, production, and markets.

The second event was that we were due for an annual audit from the corporate audit staff. The team was led by a woman who I eventually respected and a team of about 8-10 auditors. The audit would last for three months so we arranged space and housing for the team. The auditors went through their normal programs and review of processes and Six Sigma. It was getting close to the end of the audit and it was a tradition for the CFO to take the audit staff out for dinner.

We choose a nice restaurant and had the usual drinks before dinner. We continued to drink during dinner and a couple of auditors decided that they could drink me under the table. We continued drinking after dinner when we decided to go to a local night club. We continued to drink there, and by now, I was really starting to feel the effects. We all dance for a while and then I knew that I was really blitzed. It was time to go home. We went outside and were fooling around near a fountain when the *polizia* showed up. They were very unhappy about our public drunkenness and were going to take us in when Massimo jumped in and explained that he was going to take me home. I was told later that I threw up in Massimo's car and that he had to clean it up.

I felt terrible and hugged the toilet for the rest of the night and didn't go in until around ten in the morning. I was sicker than a dog and thought that I had alcohol poisoning. I spent the next couple of hours with my head down on the desk. After lunch (which I did not eat) I went over to the auditors' location to see how they were feeling. The head auditor was laughing at me and asked if I remembered the previous evening. I had to tell her no. I asked how many auditors were casualties and she indicated that all but one came into work. It was not my finest hour but at least the auditors found some humor in it. It became the event of the audit.

I just wanted to keep it quiet under the old saying of what happens on the staff stays on the staff. The audit wrapped up with no major findings and I thanked the team for their hard work. Subsequent to that dinner I stopped drinking entirely and haven't had a drink since that time.

My tenure of a little over three years was coming to a close and I was getting antsy about my next job. I also had hoped that the success of Nuovo Pignone was a catalyst to get me elected a vice-president of the company. I had gotten a call from Bob indicating that Jack wanted me to go back to a combination of the GE motors business and controls. It also had a service business. I really did not want this job especially after the success of Nuovo Pignone. I was hoping for something better than a sugar coated motors business. I was contemplating what I should do when I got a call from Bob, he listened to my concerns and then let me know that it would not be in my best interest to not accept the job that Jack wanted me to take. In addition, everyone thought it was a good assignment for me. I had to accept the position. I had survived the old fact that no first team in had ever survived but to go back to motors without being elected a vice president was disappointing.

The business gave me a really nice going away party which I had invited both Nicky (my current housekeeper and my kids former Nanny) and Massimo to attend. Some eyebrows were raised especially from the Italians who are very class conscience. I wanted everyone to meet both of them as they were as much a part of my success as was my staff. The next week the hardest part was saying goodbye to both of them. Massimo was very sad at my departure. He was like a brother to me and had sacrificed a lot.

He just never complained about any sudden changes in my schedule or the late drives home. I had bought him a Rolex as my gift goodbye and he presented me with a beautiful painting on marble by a famous artist whose previous pieces were all in a museum. It turned out that the painter was Massimo's boyhood friend and he requested him to paint a piece for me. It is still hanging in my living room and is one of my most prized possessions. Also, it is a reminder of a truly great friend. I was also allowed for any departing executive to buy their company car and have it shipped back to the states. I purchased my BMW 500 series and gave it to Nicky. That again raised a lot of questions. She was going to use it to relocate to London. I wished her goodbye. My success at Nuovo Pignone was on a large part on the ability to create a world-class finance team. They were unbelievable, and their knowledge and commitment and all the progress and presentations we made were due to them.

CHAPTER 16

Divorce

After I came back from Italy, my wife found a letter from Nicky to me (she had searched my briefcase). Of course it was a love letter. I told her that I had allowed her to return to Florida. But I didn't say that I would become a monk for three years. The fight was not a pretty sight. She was incensed. She threatened that she was going to tell all GE leadership what a dirt bag (a drunk and abusive husband) that I was; that I was having an affair with my kid's nanny and make me travel overseas with someone to watch me. I stayed the night, one eye opened, and went back to work in Indiana, which was the headquarters for GE Motors and Controls. I was really upset but realized after three years that I did not love her anymore. I loved my kids dearly but not her. I tracked Nicky down in London and found out where she was staying. I traveled to London and met Nicky. We enjoyed a long weekend together, which solidified my feelings toward her. It was simple, stay with someone who was out to ruin my career or be with someone who loved me dearly.

We were in a meeting with Jack when Dennis told him that I was getting a divorce. At the same time Dennis was also getting a divorce. He looked at both of us and said settle it out of court as he did not want another spectacle to be aired in public.

One day, I got a call from the front gate that there was somebody to see me, I told the guard to let him in. He came into my office and said, you probably know why I'm here, and slapped me with the divorce papers. He thanked me for my time and left. A divorce works only when two people can trust each other and have the children's best interest at heart. My wife, however, became a vindictive and a vitriolic woman. Every time we reached a settlement on a suit I had to pay all of her legal fees.

She was chasing judges who always favored with her as I made too much income and could afford it. When you make more than a judge does in four years they just cannot be objective. She would always serve me with papers with new issues on every birthday and holiday. Along with a request for new financial disclosure papers every time there was a new lawsuit. Most people did a lousy job on the financial statements (she never completed one). I on the other hand had to be accurate under a blanket of perjury which would impact my employment. After two years of fighting, the court demanded arbitration with a retired judge to act as an arbitrator and make sure it went smoothly.

This individual explained to me about how I would lose each subject for arbitration. His point was why argue about something that I would lose anyway. So we worked a pretty broad settlement agreement. However, we were still arguing some key points. My lawyer kept telling me that she had to leave to catch a plane. I asked her why because this was a potential settlement and a very important time in the meeting and that she should be here. About 11:30 AM, she said that she had to leave. We were so close. The next thing she said was a bombshell. She informed me that she was quitting her current firm so that she could go to work for my ex-wife's attorney and could no longer represent me. I was shocked at the obvious conflict of interest. We were just hours away from having settlement documents.

Now it was on hold until the attorneys were ready. My wife was constantly consulting with Gary Wentz's ex-wife regarding all the areas she should look for as a GE spouse (he was the President and CEO of GE Capital and his divorce was a very ugly and public event), she knew from those phone calls where all the places were that she should look for cash. We reached a settlement agreement based on the arbitration and I thought that was it. However, it would be another three years to settle all the numerous charges to be litigated. She sued over every clause that was in the agreement. My ex-wife finally had my back to the wall. I was tired of all the money issues that had been split on a fifty-fifty basis.

She never found any money that I had not documented in my financial filings. She had no reason to file any suits. Every one of the arguments, cost me more legal advice, and I would have to pay all the costs regardless if she was right or wrong. There was no downside for her. What she failed to realize was that we were only paying more money to lawyers that could be going toward the kids. I just kept looking at all the money that would not go to the children and was sick. Everything was to get even with me. My lawyer once referred her to being the most acrimonious and vindictive individual of the face of the world. The children never got a penny she even would not pay for doctor's appointments or dentists appointments even though I was paying child support.

During the arbitration, we had agreed on a total amount of alimony and child support. They came to me and asked how I would like the money divided between alimony and child support. The offer was to put more money into alimony because it would help me out as alimony was tax deductible. What I didn't realize was that there were formulas by the state on child support which were to be adhered to. So that two years later, she sued me for the back amounts due because I didn't pay the formula. This became a very big issue because they were the ones that set the allocation. I argued that it didn't matter that there were minimal payments for child support based on your income because in total she got the amount (alimony and child support) that was agreed to which was not a small amount between seven and eight thousand dollars a month. So again, I had to pay for the settlement. I was tired and beat up by the courts constantly making me pay regardless of the facts.

Another situation was on the storage unit. The stuff was allocated to me in the settlement papers as she had already gone in and taken anything of value out. All that was really in there that I wanted was my baseball cards. It turns out that she had not been paying the storage costs so all of a sudden I was hit with all the back payments and current charges. They would not deliver until the amount was paid. I refused to pay as I felt again she did not meet the spirit of the agreement. This lasted two years and again, I had to pay all the storage costs and legal fees. It had become ridiculous that the courts could not see through all these lawsuits. I was defending myself because of the principal which the Florida courts could care less about. What I should have done was sue my previous attorney for not making the first arbitration agreement bulletproof.

After four years and numerous lawsuits, the court again ordered arbitration to settle all arguments for good. During the meeting, I was so tired that I wrote down a number in cash to settle all current lawsuits and any other lawsuits in the future. After going back and forth, she agreed to the number. It cost a fortune, but I got my sanity back as this divorce and all subsequent issues took over four years to complete.

CHAPTER 17

Officer Assessment Process

Another process to become an officer of the company was an evaluation of your career going back before you entered GE and your career to date with GE. This assessment came towards the end of my tenure at Nuovo Pignone. It focused on what was important about you and what was important to GE. The three human resource executives evaluated your history including childhood and life before GE. They interviewed every one you worked with or reported to. Again, I received phone calls from friends asking what was going on and why all the questions.

They would then take all the information they collected and sit down to write an officer assessment summary. They would summarize all your strengths and weaknesses along with areas for improvements and comments on your peer reviews. After they completed the white paper, they would sit down with the individual and go through all of their conclusions and ask additional questions about your background. It was a very candid process, and it gave you immediate feedback and constructive criticism. The interview lasted about three to four hours where they could ask you any questions that they wanted to. Like so and so said this about your personality and what do you think?

Or were you proud of your father? Or what is the single greatest accomplishment of your life? Their write up of the data they collected and their opinions weighed heavily on your probability of becoming an officer of the company and for your next assignments, you can describe it as the most intense interview and deep dive into your private life that you ever had or will have. You're always evaluated based on constructive criticism, your contributions to GE, and your future potential. I thought that I would be elected as an officer, however, that call never happened.

CHAPTER 18

"Motor's Plus"

I left Nuovo Pignone toward the end of 1997. My new job was for the Motors Businesses that had some serious issues. The business was a compilation of many businesses that were close to GE motors (either by sales or cost structure or markets served). This aggregation amounted to $2.7 billion of sales with worldwide operations in thirty-three US, Mexican, and overseas components and had five thousand salaried personnel in which I was directly responsible for 350 employees. On paper, the combination of all these businesses could eliminate a lot of overlapping cost by eliminating many layers. Again I was fortunate to work with a successful driven CEO named Jim. He was a very driven man that demanded results.

The goal of these businesses was to integrate them under one roof and grow all the business while providing more service. This was a great goal and one over time could add a lot of revenues and take out a lot of excess cost. Jim would sit in his office and look at last year's sales and margins and he would look at the industry served to see if we missed any opportunities. He then would roughly take last year's business results and increase them at 10 percent growth. We would track the businesses and would visit them to understand where they were from an operating plan basis and would review current forecasts on sales and margin. Every business would indicate that it was impossible to hit those numbers they were given in sales or costs. We would review all the Six Sigma programs and how they were doing to improve processes and take out cost.

We would then go back to headquarters and he would determine each businesses operating plan. Unfortunately, the majority of earnings came from one business GE "Controls," which was tied to the production of power generation. Power Generation was in a big recession and the controls budget should have been tied to the budget for power generation. Regardless, we gave them a challenge to hit their budget. After we prepared all the budgets, we would then review them with the businesses, listen to their concerns and give them their budgets. This methodology was flawed to begin with as some of the businesses just could not achieve growth because of the recession. So out of the block we would miss our commitment to the company and at the same time, we were in the process of moving the headquarters to Atlanta, Georgia, from Fort Wayne, Indiana.

Here's where it always got dicey. I was told not to communicate to corporate until Jim gave the chairman a heads-up. We were responsible to give finance primarily Jack's vice president of Financial Planning and Analysis (Bob) a realistic update. By the time I was "allowed" to communicate to corporate, it would be too late. The

Corporate FP&A group and specifically Bob were saddled with getting all the business numbers and where there was a shortfall to get the income from another business so that we would not miss our commitment to Wall Street.

There were operation reviews every quarter. The first was the CEOs quarterly business review where he pitched the quarterly financials (which was where we stood on hitting our commitments), along with an update on Six Sigma. The CFOs also held a quarterly operating review with Dennis Dammerman and his staff (update on hitting quarterly numbers). Finance knew that there was no way we were going to hit our commitments but our presentation matched the CEOs presentation. Realistically, the estimates of operations considered the actuals for two months and projected one month's estimate. It would be a very close representation of where the business was financially. Why we couldn't just own up was so very damaging to credibility especially mine.

At the CFO meetings, you were hit with two ramifications. First is missing your commitment and the second was the lack of a timely heads-up. This situation created conflict between the CEO of the business and CFO, the latter always trying to communicate reality to corporate, the former always trying to drive the business for results to the last day, so as far as he was concerned we were still on budget/estimate.

We were pitching to Jack our session 2 held in September with total year operations with two quarters in the bag. We had just finished an operating review and now all the growth was in the last quarter. Jim wanted Jack to know that I had just had my appendix taken out two days ago. He wanted them to know my level of commitment and sacrifice. Jim pitched the introduction of the business and strategic and operational progress followed by my presentation of the financials.

Jack had already flipped through the presentation and knew the questions he wanted to ask. He had an incredible understanding of the business and markets and what in the budget it would be difficult to achieve. The meeting went okay but you could still see he was preoccupied with something else. At the end of the presentation, he asked Jim to have lunch with him. It was Dennis who informed me that our CEO had been removed. On the way back, Jim confided that he had been fired but was given a generous separation package. He also informed us not to worry as corporate did not have any problems with either of us.

We continued to do our jobs until new opportunities came up (compiling results in operations along with updated business plans) it was also clear that the business had to be integrated. The entire business was given to Electrical Distribution and Controls. That business had an excellent CFO who had recently been appointment a vice-president, so in essence I was on the outside looking in.

CHAPTER 19

IT Solutions

At one of Denice's quarterly reviews, we had a guest speaker from GE Capital to talk about this great business and all the growth and productivity that they were doing. The audience was enamored with the presentation and everybody wanted to know more. No one was asking is this real? And given the up lift it had on the audience no one wanted to ask any negative questions. Unfortunately, I remembered this CFO and presentation as I was about to take over as the CFO of this business six months later. My understanding was that they were doing an operations review of GE Capital and on a recently acquired business that provided $8.5 billion in revenues. This was an IT product and service business and included operations in the US, Mexico, Canada, Brazil, Germany, and Australia employing thirteen thousand employees globally.

Jack looked across the table and asked them if anybody had visited the businesses as it was recently acquired or even understood exactly what they did as each business had a different business proposition. The answer was not encouraging. Jack looked down the table to Dennis and asked where I was and if I was available as I had just finished two years previously a successful integration of Nouvo Pignone. Dennis responded that I was in Atlanta, Georgia, and available. He just said good get him to Minneapolis (the headquarters of this joint venture and of these businesses).

This was unusual as GE Capital did not have any industrial CFOs. Jack was pissed that the business was allowed to buy a compilation of businesses this large without having deeper reviews of the acquired businesses.

I went to Minneapolis, Minnesota (unbelievable because it was really a brutal environment). I got temporary housing and a rental car and went to the headquarters. Unfortunately, the majority of the businesses had different platforms and it was problematic to consolidate all of them. Therefore, the financials weren't available until after the closing event, at that point we could review the financials and ask questions. The next day, I started to look at all the businesses. It became clear that the Minneapolis facility was the largest of the businesses. In the past, they would purchase computers at a lower cost than the public by using volume discounts. They would then go to the customer and install the computers. There was little services portion of the business as it was just the initial installation.

However, with the advent of Dell computers and the ability to supply businesses directly you knew that the margins which were once 15 percent were going to single digits. You can't cut enough people to offset the margin decline (been there done that) from there I went to each of the businesses (along with the business that we bought from John Ramsey). Some served a market with just computers while others had product sales and service contracts for any product sold. I spent quite a lot of my Minneapolis time discussing the business and markets with the president and CEO (Steve) of the US (Box) business. He came across at first like slick Willy, but with time, he was a very intelligent man with a gift for communication and motivating organizations. We discussed where we thought the market would go, what size of the market we would wind up with, and the profitability of that business.

We immediately began developing a restructuring plan, which included consolidating the headquarters operations from Stamford Connecticut and Minneapolis to Cincinnati, Ohio.

The CEO of this new business was the past CFO of the Lighting Business (Jim). It wasn't going to be pleasant task going back to Jack and telling him that the largest company of this compilation of businesses was in the US and would soon be a thing of the past unless they could create a real service business. The service contracts would follow the product and also maintain the systems for the schools, military, colleges, corporations, etc. Canada sold product service contracts. So did the German operation. All these businesses could be saved with more service margins. We then talked about the ability to gain opportunities and challenges.

I set out to build a world class finance team from the various parts of the business and corporate candidates. We then all moved to Cincinnati to our new headquarters. We began to put the various plans together to integrate the businesses and the restructuring that would be required.

The issue was that the restructuring plan was not enough reduction in costs to offset declining sales and margins. It is always tough restructuring, especially in a business that has declining sales, everyone always screams that they can't take out anymore costs (personnel). We also determined what companies to sell.

During one of Jim's monthly operations review the manager of the Mexico business could not explain the difference in cash flow as it related to the balance sheet. I kept asking questions, and he kept saying different responses. I stopped because this was starting to be too embarrassing for him in front of his peers. It always amazed me that in reviews, no one ever followed the cash. If you were doing things right, the earnings of the business operations should have some relation to the cash flow. If it didn't you would need to go deep to find out what was wrong.

You need to do a deep review to determine if the net income is due to operations or from balance sheet adjustments.

Separately, I had a routine that I always followed in every previous business to eliminate year-end surprises. Somewhere around the middle of November, I would hold a year-end closing meeting. This was a ritual for me and gave me a chance to review the last month estimates, the balance sheet and any business issues that needed to be addressed before we got into the closing week. It was important that with eleven months of the year gone that they could estimate accurately what was going to happen in the last four weeks. We went from business to business and then it was Mexico's turn. The business had sent the controller of the business and not the CFO. I kept asking questions as the numbers just didn't make sense, again especially cash flow. About halfway through the presentation, she started crying.

I indicated that we had been going strong since morning and we should take a break and reconvene in twenty minutes. I met the controller out in the hallway and asked if everything was okay, she said no. Then she continued to tell me that the records wouldn't tie because they had paid a rather sizable bribe to get a large order. My mind went to overdrive on the severity of this situation this close to year end and the number of people I had to bring up to speed. In addition, I immediately sent a team down to understand who knew what and when. Turns out that they had all gone to lunch where the topic of the day was what kind of luggage should we get to carry the money! Unfortunately, the young lady that came forward had to be fired with the CEO, CFO, and controller. I was disappointed about the affair because of all the conversations we had on doing the business the right way. We were able to fix the damage and prepared a presentation for the Mexico government as to what had gone wrong and the remedial actions we were taking.

Our German business was the hardest to restructure as it hit its forecasted business margins and cash flow. The German operation listened to the proposed Business plan for sales, margins and the amount of restructuring that needed to take place. They agreed that they would return to Germany and execute the plan set in place. Unfortunately; the business leader had no intention of doing any restructuring. They would completely ignore the plan from headquarters even though they agreed to implement it. During the first quarter, I traveled to Germany and let them tell me what they could agree to execute.

The issue was that the CEO would say the right words on implementing the plans given to them and I would then leave to go back to the US. He would then promptly not implement the agreed-upon restructure and tell the employees that they didn't need corporate to tell them how to run their business. I recommended that the CEO be replaced and If that wasn't possible, to sell the German operation. This recommendation was not implemented.

We continued with operating all the components and guiding them through their restructuring plans. The reality though was that the US business was losing profitability and that costs could not be reduced fast enough to keep up with falling revenues. This created a big problem for the business which the other components could not make up. We were also determining which businesses to sell. We would hold monthly reviews with GE Capital. These reviews would be with Gary Wendt's operation leader and the CFO of GE Capital, Jim P. Both were very talented executives with many years of experience and insights their input was important for success. On occasion, Gary Wendt would attend the reviews and focus more on how to grow the business both in sales and service. He was more strategically focused than operational. He had an interesting habit during business reviews. He drank his coffee in a Styrofoam cup and when finished would begin eating the cup one small piece at a time. It was distracting to say the least. Gary had built GE Capital into a significant business that was a large part of GE's net income. He was very proud of his achievements and very independent. Jack had the insight to explain to analyst's that the thirteen industrial business generated significant cash flow that financed GE Capital's ability to perform acquisitions. GE Capital was like a very tightly controlled business that acquired many companies both domestically and internationally that generated a lot of net income.

At the same time, we were having a lot of operations reviews with another GE co-chairman named John. We reviewed with him because of the restructuring that we were implementing and the fact that he used to be Jim's boss at Lighting.

He would review our plans and the timing and then give us feedback and direction. We continued to restructure the businesses and also to get them on a common reporting platform so that it didn't take so long to consolidate the monthly and quarterly results. Because of all the different accounting platforms we were always the last business to report. I was busting my ass traveling to all the businesses, consolidating the accounting platforms, and restructuring the businesses or putting into plans which businesses to sell. Every time we turned around we were meeting with either Jack, GE Capital, or John. My boss was coming under increasingly more pressure to execute the business plan.

We were at this point in restructuring the operations when I got a phone call from the past US president, Steve, who I mentioned earlier. He had left GE to become president and COO of a startup company that had some significant investment money, from both the public, private equity and debt financing. He was talking about how great the public sector was and all the investors that had invested in the business (large businesses including Enron and Cisco). It sounded like he was having a really good time. It was then that I started thinking about leaving GE for the experience of operating a total finance operation. My background and experiences made me a very good candidate to some company.

GE had made me a senior vice president in GE Capital but that was not the same as being promoted to a vice president in the company. Every year, the headquarters, high potential employees, and employees that had made a significant contribution were taken for a week-long trip to a very nice place. It was first class. The CEOs generally included their CFO's as a thank-you for all the hard work. This was the first trip that I didn't go on and I couldn't understand why. Each business was given the number of people who could attend. I had gone to Hawaii the year before and felt comfortable that I would be selected, but this would not be the case.

About this time, I was being heavily recruited by Steve to join the company that he had left for. A publicly held business in Denver, Colorado, called Rhythms NetConnections. I had worked out a package that would match what I was getting today in GE (cash plus stock options). They did not want me to shop the contract and then negotiate to stay in GE as it was pretty lucrative. I had really enjoyed working with Steve and also liked the chairman of the company. I gave the offer and the business preposition a lot of consideration. I decided to go to the new company to get the total experience of running a total finance operation including the relationships with bankers, investors, public accounting firms, and taxing authorities. I faxed my letter of resignation to my boss.

I really thought they would do everything to attempt to keep me. But it went radio silent. Dennis asked the CEO what the issue was and what I wanted, as he already had made me a senior vice president in GE Capital. My boss was starting an excuse for not executing our business plan that would cover his ass as he had failed to execute the restructuring plans. He blamed the finance organization. He made the excuse that finance had not given him the right financials to make decisions and that was probably the real reason I was leaving. It was after I had left that I heard employees in the business and leadership positions that Jack was surprised by the allegations and ask a couple of his senior people to find out what was going on. After reviewing all the plans and financials they reported back that all the available financials and recommendations were available and that my ex-CEO had plenty of current financials and monthly business reports, status of restructuring progress, and variances to plans to run the business. After reporting their findings to Jack, he called my ex-boss to Fairfield where he was terminated.

I had a lot of experiences at GE and wanted to build my own financial operations also, a lot of people were making millions in startup companies. It was coming close to when Jack and Dennis would be retiring and Jack's replacement being announced. I felt that with the new leadership team my support group was diminishing and I had to network. So my GE career was over and I appreciated all the opportunities and support that the company had given me. It was a great ride.

CHAPTER 20

Concluding Thoughts

My concluding thoughts and lessons of experience.

Develop and maintain your networking both externally and internally. Also, develop appropriate mentors and support of current business leaders as they routinely talk about the top finance people.

GE was a numbers business. You hit your commitments. If you were not going to hit them then continue over communicating what is really going to happen.

Even if you went "off the record," there wasn't too many people that could have received "an off the record's financials," without feeling the need to communicate to someone else and this creates a tremendous strain between the CEO and CFO. Over communicate to your business (and CEO) what you feel the need to communicate.

Don't be afraid to jump on new initiatives to keep you up-to-date on new ideas. Also, if you see something that you think will benefit your business. Don't be afraid to "steal it."

Learn the best practices of each leader in the business and other businesses as these will always be mentors and a networking group. Make the time to talk with them as this is critical to your development. Build your leadership style by taking the leadership teams best practices and ignoring the bad. Every business leader has good and bad styles.

Don't sell yourself short, every move I made was a jump into the deep end of the pool and I always found out that I could exceed. There is no failure if you try, there's only failure if you don't try.

Stress kills. It is critical to balance your work/life. Find a way to release your stress, a hobby, spending time with the kids, leaving your office building for a short walk, anything that will work for you. If you want to have a retirement, you'll find a way.

Your career seems like a long time, but it goes quickly. Find a way to love what you do so that every day is a joy to go into work. If you're miserable, it will show and permeate throughout the organization.

Hire the best people that you can. Fill your organization with high potential individuals and direct them on what you expect. Then turn them loose.

Remember, I will learn from my past, use lessons learned for the present and apply both for the future.

ABOUT THE AUTHOR

John W Braukman III (Jay) was born in Covington, Kentucky. He graduated from Seminole High School in Seminole, Florida, and then the University of Cincinnati (UC). Jay then joined General Electric's (GE's) Financial Management Program, Corporate Audit Staff, and then a very successful twenty-three-year career in various financial and sales management positions before becoming the chief financial officer (CFO) of four major GE businesses. He then left GE to become a senior vice-president and CFO of a startup DSL Company and then a senior vice president, chief operating officer (COO) and CFO in the Telecommunications Industry as well as a senior vice-president and CFO in the Food Industry and Information Technology Product and Services.

He attended all three of GE's Executive Development Programs and has served on a number of board of directors' positions. In May 2011, he received his master of business administration in management from the Florida Institute of Technology (FIT). Jay lives in Tarpon Springs, Florida, with his wife Nicky and has four children, Shelly, John, Lauren, and Matteo as well as five grandchildren. He enjoys golf, fishing, and raising, breeding, and showing French bulldogs. He currently has three very spoiled "Frenchies" Bella, Luna, and Sunny. He enjoys college sports and hopes that UC will again win a National Championship. In 1972, he was commissioned a Kentucky Colonel in the Commonwealth of Kentucky.

www.ingramcontent.com/pod-product-compliance
Lightning Source LLC
Chambersburg PA
CBHW030945180526
45163CB00002B/706